GUT-CHECK

YOUR PRIME SOURCE FOR BOWEL HEALTH AND COLON CANCER PREVENTION

GUT-CHECK

YOUR PRIME SOURCE FOR BOWEL HEALTH AND COLON CANCER PREVENTION

by

Jeffrey M. Aron, M.D.
Harriette Aron

ISBN: 0-75960-498-3

This book is printed on acid free paper.

1stBooks - rev. 9/26/01

TABLE OF CONTENTS

INTRODUCTION

INTRODUCTION

"Doc, I can't get out the gas," the man exclaimed, his eyes bulging and teeth clenched. "No matter how hard I try, I can't get out the gas!" Howard, a successful business executive, looked as if he were about to explode as he explained that he could only eat baby food because of his terrible gas and abdominal pain.

Then there was Brad, a very anxious young college student, who was trying to cope with the fear surrounding his father's newly diagnosed colon cancer. "Should I be concerned about getting colon cancer, Dr. Aron? Do I need to be tested? What can I do to prevent colon cancer?" These were just a few of his many questions.

Sarah, a yoga instructor from Berkeley, is another interesting patient with an intriguing question. "Dr. Aron, is it all right if I detox my system with a coffee enema? Everyone I know is doing it, and they say it's great for cleansing your body. What do you think?"

On the phone is Lisa, a young mother of two, who I saw several years ago as a patient. "Dr. Aron, I'm calling for my best friend Cynthia. She thinks she has the same problem with her bowels that I had, but she's too embarrassed to talk to her doctor. What was that medicine you prescribed to me, she wants to know."

Howard, Brad, Sarah, and Lisa are typical of the patients I've seen over the past three decades as a practicing gastroenterologist. During this time as a teacher, researcher, and practitioner I have been asked thousands of questions like these and have observed how every aspect of ones' health is affected by their bowel function.

I believe that your bowel movements represent the end result of how you live, eat, breathe, relax, love, and feel about yourself and others.

I have also observed that due to their fear of embarrassment many people lack a basic understanding of bowel function and its relationship to their overall optimal health. People often feel too ashamed to openly discuss their bowel problems, saying they have the "stomach flu" or "indigestion" rather than admitting their real problem is their bowel movements. This attitude is understandable, since most of our references to elimination have been relegated to the realm of sophomoric bathroom humor by our society. Even in childhood, the first terms for elimination are taught to us in slang language, instilling the idea that the appropriate words are just too embarrassing to say. It is a serious mistake to dismiss this crucial body function with a few jokes and allow the fear of embarrassment to keep you from seeking the advice you need.

Over the years, many patients have asked me for a single resource to help them with their bowel problems, and, with my wife and co-author Harriette, I have written this book to provide you with the latest expert advice on complete bowel care.

This book is a concise, easy-to-use source of information based on my professional experience and the most authoritative scientific research on how to optimize bowel function, achieve great health, and prevent disease.

The book is divided into five parts. In the first section, EMBARRASSMENT, MYTH, AND MIND I share with you three patient histories that will provide a new insight into your bowel care. The first history explores the embarrassment so many people feel when trying to discuss their bowel problems. You will learn how once a patient's fear is overcome she is able to speak openly about her problem and, with my recommendations, begins the healing process.

There are also many myths surrounding bowel care based on folklore and homespun remedies. In our second patient history we debunk one of these popular myths concerning laxative use and alert you to its potential hidden dangers.

The third case history addresses the mind-to-bowel relationship. This is a vital yet often overlooked influence on bowel health. In this history a patient's traumatic childhood experience is revealed to him as the source of his abdominal pain, and by making this connection he is able to overcome a lifelong problem.

The second section, A JOURNEY THROUGH YOUR BOWELS, follows an imaginary meal through your digestive system. With an easy-to-follow diagram, we guide you through each process involved in your bowel function. I believe you will come away with a complete understanding of what a bowel movement is and why it is so essential to your overall health.

In part three, ANSWERS TO SOME OF LIFE'S MOST EMBARRASSING QUESTIONS, I answer a wide range of questions on bowel health. From the most frequently asked questions such as "How many bowel movements a day is normal?" to the most embarrassing questions such as "Why does gas smell" and "How does anal sex affect bowel movements?" I answer these questions with straightforward advice, a touch of humor, and the most authoritative scientific research in both traditional and alternative medicine.

Some of the topics discussed include:

- BOWEL MOVEMENTS
- CONSTIPATION
- DIARRHEA
- GAS
- COLON CANCER
- LACTOSE INTOLERANCE
- COLON CLEANSING
- EATING DISORDERS
- ANAL SEX
- WEIGHT CONTROL
- DIABETES
- ENEMAS
- AGING
- IRRITABLE BOWEL SYNDROME

Plus many other important areas of concern.

The fourth section addresses the growing problem of COLORECTAL CANCER. Many people are surprised to learn that this cancer is the second most common cancer in our society, with the average person having a 1 in 16 chance of developing it in their lifetime. This section focuses on the intimate relationship between bowel function and colorectal cancer, and discusses how genetic and environmental factors can influence the development of polyps and cancer. It summarizes the history of the evolution of our current knowledge on how to prevent this disease, and gives clear guidelines on when to use colonoscopy to detect and remove polyps before they become cancers. I provide a summary of recommendations for dietary, lifestyle, and supplement use that lower your risk for developing colorectal cancer and are part of the BOWEL CARE AND COLON CANCER PREVENTION PLAN.

Part five is THE BOWEL CARE AND COLON CANCER PREVENTION PLAN. Here I present a simple four-part plan that works. It includes diet, fluids, exercise, and relaxation techniques that will have your bowels working smoothly in 10 to

14 days. Moreover, this plan lowers the risk for developing colon cancer significantly with additional benefits to your overall health. The plan has been designed as an easy-to-use guide to assist you in making informed choices which can be incorporated into your daily routine. In each part of the plan you will find specific recommendations with helpful tips that emphasize moderation, flexibility, and variety. I can appreciate that when a plan or diet is too rigid, we are less likely to follow it for long. That is why I've created a plan that you can live with on a day-to-day basis throughout your life, because I want you to reap all the benefits the plan has to offer. We've also provided a full week of customized menus to give you some workable ideas on how you can have meals that are delicious, healthy, and within our guidelines and recommendations.

This book was written to supply you with the knowledge to take control of your bowel care as a well-informed, active participant. We hope this book gives you the confidence to stop being embarrassed, alleviate unnecessary suffering, and maximize your health potential.

CHAPTER I

EMBARRASEMENT, MYTH AND MIND

CHAPTER I

EMBARRASSMENT, MYTH, AND MIND

In learning about bowel function and understanding the major role it plays in your health, it's important to first address the matters of embarrassment, myth, and mind. These three elements are commonly neglected but are an essential link to diagnosing and treating bowel dysfunction.

I know that having a relaxed and open dialogue on this difficult subject is not easy. Society has always regarded the discussion of bowel movements as taboo, placing it in the context of bathroom humor. Of course, a good dose of humor is often the very best medicine when discussing bowel movements and their inevitable companion, flatulence.

Over the years I have observed that even in the privacy of the doctor's office people feel uncomfortable and are greatly embarrassed when discussing their bowel problems.

EMBARRASSMENT

I can recall the time when a young female executive came to see me because of abdominal pain. Laura walked into my office, very anxious and nervous, carrying her briefcase, computer, and cell phone. We discussed her abdominal pain in some detail, and I began to inquire about her daily life: What foods did she eat? How many hours of sleep did she get? Did she exercise? She answered these questions easily, except when I asked about her bowel movements and gas. She suddenly lowered her head and looked sheepishly up at me. "That's my real problem," she said. "I can't go out in public without the need to pass gas. The worst time is when I'm in a crowded elevator, or conducting a meeting. I become so panicked about passing gas that when I'm in a restroom I'm afraid to pass it!" I could see Laura's embarrassment, and I told her most women won't admit to passing gas, but men seem to revel in their prowess at this ability, often speaking with real pride about their many "accomplishments," such as how high their emission would measure on the Richter scale. This little story made her laugh, and we talked about how it's normal to pass gas several times a day and even at night during sleep. We could now discuss Laura's real problem without her feeling embarrassed, and although this type of problem may seem trivial or humorous, it was seriously affecting her quality of life.

Laura's daily routine, as you might guess, was a hectic schedule of business meetings and answering e-mail, voice mail, and pages. She was busy making herself available to everyone but herself. She didn't take the time to relax, eat right, or drink enough fluids. Sound familiar? I must see at least one new patient like her every day. I explained to her that making a few easy adjustments in her daily routine was all she needed. By taking some time to relax, adding fiber to her diet, and increasing her fluid intake Laura's pain and gas problems would lessen in a month and gradually disappear.

MYTH

There are many misconceptions people have about their bowel movements and bowel functions. Cures that are handed down in families or well-intentioned advice from friends are generally the main source of this misinformation. I have noticed that even the most sophisticated and knowledgeable people can lack a basic understanding of their bowels and often confuse myth with fact.

A perfect example of this was Martha, a mature independent woman with constipation and abdominal pain who you will meet again later in this book. In her profession, Martha traveled extensively and always ate in restaurants and hotels. She exercised and was diligent about her fluid and fiber intake, but despite this she still had a constipation problem. She ate prunes every day and took an herbal cleansing formula for relief. In the beginning this was successful but as time passed, she had to use increasing amounts of the prunes and herbal formulas in order to have **any** bowel movements. Martha believed that because they were natural they would be safe no matter how much or how long she used them.

Nothing could have been further from the truth, yet I can't tell you how many people I have seen who believe this. In fact, she was repeatedly injuring her colon. Upon colonoscoping her I found the most advanced case of "laxative abuse colon" I had ever seen. The prunes and the herbs found in the cleansing formula are known to contain compounds that are actual irritants to the colon. Once these were eliminated from her system and she was placed on a program of diet, fluid, relaxation, exercise, and safe laxatives, her bowel movements returned to normal. Martha learned what laxatives were safe to use in an appropriate manner and that just because something is natural doesn't mean that it can't be harmful.

MIND

Another important aspect too often neglected by patients and their physicians is the mind-to-bowel relationship. I'm sure many of you are thinking "what could my mind have to do with my bowel movements?" The answer is everything. From the time of conception your mind and bowel have developed together, exchanging between them information that affects each of them. There are intimate, intricate, and complex linkages between the mind and the bowel which make the bowel and your bowel movements especially vulnerable to dysfunction. Your awareness of your bowel movements and bowel functions is greatly influenced by life experiences. Experiences ranging from how you were toilet trained to psychological, physical, or sexual abuse and your early eating patterns, all serve to modify the interaction between your mind and your bowel. Many of these experiences have occurred in your childhood and may have been repressed, while others currently exist but remain unconfronted.

One such example was when a very stressed man in his thirties came to see me about his "ulcer disease." Jim told me he had consulted other physicians who had run a series of tests and x-rays which were negative. He was also given medications for ulcer disease that had little effect. Jim's pain occurred soon after eating and caused him to feel bloated and nauseated with a discomfort in his abdomen. I asked him questions about his daily routine and about his bowel movements. Jim was very surprised about these questions and began to tell me that his bowel movements had been a major problem all his life. As a child, his mother expected him to have a bowel movement before he was allowed to leave for school. She believed that he had to "cleanse" his bowels every day. She would even go so far as to administer enemas to him when he was unable to eliminate (what a horrible, traumatic experience for a child!). I'm sure those of you who have experienced an enema as a child will agree that it's something one never forgets. I was the first person he had ever confided in about this experience, and he had been living his life burdened with this distorted view.

I told Jim that many people have a misguided view of having to cleanse oneself every day or even after every meal. There are many psychological issues involved in why people believe this, none of which have anything to do with cleansing. I continued to discuss with him how over time he had been oversensitized to the sensations in his rectum and lower colon that occur normally after meals.

It was easy to understand how many of the doctors Jim consulted believed that his symptoms were associated with an ulcer, but this was not the case. Recent research has demonstrated in patients similar to Jim that an increase in abnormal brain activity makes patients exquisitely more aware of their rectum and colon, and that repeated stimulation of one area to the bowels can lead to increased sensitivity in other areas of the body. Those feelings of pain and discomfort in his stomach were real but were not the source of his problem.

I started Jim on a program with a prescription medication that slows the huge volume of nerve traffic from his bowel to his brain, and also improves the brain's processing of that information. I told him to expect sensations of bloating and fullness after meals that could occur occasionally, but not to be concerned about them as they did not signify any illness. Diet, relaxation, and exercise would also help to normalize his bowel sensitivity. Eventually, Jim was able to stop all medications and began to take control of his life, his bowel movements, and his health for the first time.

This patient's story serves as a good example of how the mind-to-bowel relationship works and how it can affect your overall health. So many patients tell me they begin to feel better immediately, just by being aware of this connection. In my many years as a physician, I have found nothing more gratifying than helping someone discover the origins and causes of their illness and to give them the help they need.

CHAPTER II

A JOURNEY THROUGH YOUR BOWELS

CHAPTER II

A JOURNEY THROUGH YOUR BOWELS

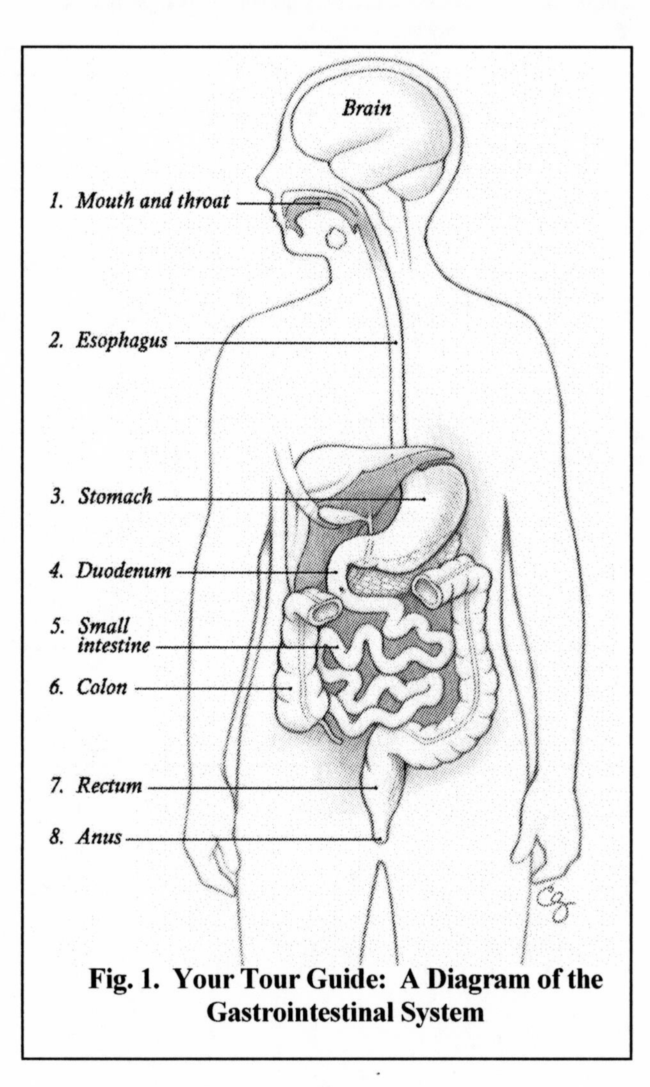

Fig. 1. Your Tour Guide: A Diagram of the Gastrointestinal System

Brain and nervous system	Sends and receives messages throughout the entire process
1) Mouth and Throat	Food is chewed and mixed with saliva for swallowing
2) Esophagus	Food is propelled down this muscular tube to the stomach
3) Stomach	Food is churned and mixed with stomach acid, then broken down for delivery to the duodenum
4) Duodenum	Bile from the liver and enzymes from the pancreas combine to prepare the food for absorption by the small intestine
5) Small Intestine	Most food is absorbed is absorbed and delivered by blood vessels and lymph channels to the body. The remainder is delivered to the colon where it becomes stool
6) Colon	Fiber in the food forms solid stool and tones the muscles of the colon which move it into the rectum
7) Rectum	Stool is collected here before expulsion
8) Anus	Controls passage of stool out of the body

A JOURNEY THROUGH YOUR BOWELS

Do you know what a bowel movement really is? Most people don't know—they just assume it is something that they pass and flush away. But a bowel movement is much more: It is the final result of one of the most important and complex functions of the body. It's how the body eliminates your wastes and toxins, and regulates your metabolic, hormonal, immune, and nervous functions. We want to take you on a journey through your bowels to show you how the food you consume is processed into forming a bowel movement. This will give you a basic understanding of what a bowel movement is and why it is important to your overall health.

STEP 1: THE MOUTH AND THROAT

This is the first step of your food's journey. Here, the food is ground and mixed with saliva, breaking it down to be swallowed. At this point, the flavor, texture, and aroma of your food signal the brain, which helps to prepare the rest of the digestive tract to receive the food.

STEP 2: THE ESOPHAGUS

The food arrives here after it is swallowed. The muscles of the esophagus relax and contract in an orderly and coordinated fashion to propel the food to the stomach.

STEP 3: THE STOMACH

The stomach is divided into the upper and lower sections, each with a separate function. Your food has now entered the upper stomach where:

- Muscles act like a piston to push the food to the lower stomach, and at the same time stomach acid is added in just the right amount to the food to start digestion

The food is now delivered into the lower stomach where:

- Muscles knead and grind the food into very small pieces which are then delivered into the duodenum
- The stomach muscles are stretched, sending a message to the brain of satisfaction and comfortable fullness

STEP 4: THE DUODENUM

As the food particles are delivered in the duodenum these activities occur:

- The duodenum receives bile from the liver and enzymes from the pancreas to digest fat, protein, and carbohydrate, and prepares them for absorption by the small intestine
- Bile removes cholesterol from the blood stream
- Hormonal messages are released to control the utilization of the food by the body
- Messages are sent to the brain and the rest of the intestine to control appetite, mood, and continue digestion

STEP 5: THE SMALL INTESTINE

Most of the food is absorbed here, and once absorbed it is delivered to the rest of the body. The remainder of the food, especially fiber, is delivered to the colon to form stool.

STEP 6: THE COLON

The fiber in the food tones the muscles and provides energy for the colon. It forms the stool so that the colonic muscles can move it smoothly into the rectum.

STEP 7: THE RECTUM

The stool collects here, and once the collection becomes large enough to stretch the rectal wall, signals are sent to your nervous system, making you aware of the urge to eliminate waste.

STEP 8: THE ANUS

This is the final step of your food's journey through your bowels. It is the place from which your stool exits your body.

STEP 9: THE BRAIN AND NERVOUS SYSTEM

At every step on this journey, your brain and nervous system have interacted with your bowels by sending and receiving messages throughout the entire body. Some of these messages are the taste, texture, and aroma of food, the sensation of stomach fullness, and the sensing of the need to eliminate waste.

CHAPTER III

ANSWERS TO SOME OF LIFE'S MOST EMBARRASSING QUESTIONS

CHAPTER III

ANSWERS TO SOME OF LIFE'S MOST EMBARRASSING QUESTIONS

ANSWERS TO QUESTIONS ON BOWEL MOVEMENTS

How many bowel movements a day are normal?

Between three motions a day to three a week is the range of normal stool frequency. In general, this is a pretty good rule of thumb, but like every generalization some modifiers are important:

- The b.m. should be easy to pass, without having to strain.
- The motion should have form or shape, but be soft
- No pain associated with passing the stool
- You should not be awakened from sleep in order to have a bowel movement.

How long should a bowel movement take?

I'm sure that this question has plagued many people, especially those who live with others, and where there is only one available toilet. The problem is compounded by the widely-held and most definitely mythical belief that one must have a complete evacuation every time that one is seated upon the "throne"!

Really, it is not important that one hits a home run every time at bat, or scores a touchdown every time one carries the ball! Sometimes a walk or a single, or even a good gain should be adequate. The idea that a complete evacuation has to happen every time that one feels the urge leads many to sit and force the stool out, no matter what. Having repeated anxiety over the sense of incomplete evacuation can lead to many other problems, such as the irritable bowel syndrome.

This also causes excessive tension in the pelvic muscles that form the supporting structures of the anus, and can lead to fissures, bleeding, and hemorrhoids. Most bowel movements should be completed within five to ten minutes. If **every** b.m. takes longer than this then there is a problem, such as not sitting properly on the toilet, reading, or basic inadequacies with diet, fluid, exercise, and the ability to relax.

I know many patients seek the quietude of the bathroom, as the last refuge of privacy and peace. Lately, however, laptop and palmtop computers have broken into this sanctum, causing their fascinated users to sit there for an eternity while "surfing the net" during defecation. I have also seen patients who take the New York Times crossword puzzle into the toilet every day, and not leave until they have completed it! All of these practices are to be avoided if one is to have normal b.m.'s.

Is it all right to read on the toilet?

This question, believe it or not, has fostered considerable debate among gastroenterologists and proctologists. One camp holds that all reading on the can is abnormal, while another argues that reading on the toilet seat helps to relax the individual.

As with any polemic, a compromise view is probably correct. When one reads while seated on the "throne" there is a tendency to lean forward, resting the elbows on the knees, holding the object being read in the hands. Leaning forward in such a manner produces an acute angle between the anal canal and the rectum. This forces the stool from the rectum to be propelled against the wall of the anus instead of being given a "straight shot" through the axis of the anal canal into the waiting toilet bowl beneath.

In addition, such positioning places weight more forward on the balls of the feet, destabilizing the floor of the pelvis and producing excessive tension, which further impedes easy passage of the stool.

However, there is something to be said about properly relaxing to commence the b.m. So, it is all right to read on the toilet seat for the first few minutes but not throughout the entire b.m.

There are some who take reading on the toilet seat to an extreme. One patient, a medical student, no less, read all of the current medical journals while so seated! Needless to say, he had similar complaints of excessive gas, incomplete evacuations, and intermittent bleeding from anal fissures.

So, if you must read, read a little at the start of the bowel movement, put the reading material aside, plant your feet squarely on the floor, and finish the b.m. Finish your reading somewhere else that is more appropriate.

I find myself uncomfortable on many of the toilets that I have to use at times. Is there a right way of sitting on the toilet?

There certainly is. One must be able to plant one's feet comfortably flat on the floor. Just having the toes touching the floor is inadequate. Sit straight, leaning slightly forward at the waist. If the toilet seat is too low then you can use a booster. If, on the other hand, your feet do not reach the floor then a platform may be used.

Leaning forward when your feet are not flat on the floor or when reading will cause an acute angle between your rectum and anus, so that when the stool is being expelled it comes directly up against the anus, causing a tear, or fissure.

Sometimes I feel like I cannot completely evacuate my stool. Why?

There are many reasons for this problem. Most commonly, there is excessive tension in the pelvic muscles that surround the anus and rectum. This tension is a reflection of the generalized stress of daily living. Some people have the problem of clenching their jaw muscles and grinding their teeth, others place tension in their pelvic muscles.

You can learn to relax your pelvic muscles by taking a warm tub bath each evening. First, fill the tub with water that is just slightly warm, and sit with the water up to your waist. Relax, listen to some music, light some aromatic candles, or read an enjoyable book. Take some deep breaths for about fifteen minutes. Do this for a week, then taper down to two or three times a week as your symptoms improve. Over a long period, a bath like this once or twice a week will keep your pelvic muscles adequately relaxed. You'll probably sleep better, as well.

Some stretching or yoga positions are also helpful to relax these muscles. Sit on the floor with your back straight. Put the soles of your feet together and hold both hands around the toes. Then, bring your knees together, keep your back straight, and take in a deep breath. Hold it for ten to fifteen seconds, then gently exhale while letting your knees fall gently to the side. Repeat this sequence three times. Try to do this daily.

Other significant causes of the sense of incomplete evacuation should be explored by your doctor. These include the inability of the wall of the rectum to relax after defecation, a reflection of increased tension in the wall of the rectum. While this can be caused by inadequate fiber and fluid in the diet and inadequate relaxation, wall tension can be increased by inflammation, growths, or scarring in the tissues that comprise the rectal wall. These should be explored with your doctor, who can begin a careful evaluation of your problem with a complete history and examination that includes a rectal exam.

Is it harmful to resist the urge to defecate?

There are occasions in all of our lives that are marked by an inopportune time to have a b.m. If you have to go and there is no rest room available, or if you are in the middle of an important meeting, then you must try to suck it up, tighten up, and pray!

On these occasions, you might be successful in holding back the tide for a few more minutes, and possibly as long as even an hour, but, over time, you'll eventually have to give in. If you have to go through this only on rare occasions then no harm will occur. On the other hand, if you do this frequently you can almost guarantee future problems with hemorrhoids, gas, constipation, and anal fissures.

I get pains in my rectum at certain times when I have a bowel movement. Should I worry about this?

Everyone, once in a while, experiences pain upon defecation; it is when you feel pain on more than two successive b.m.'s that you may have a problem.

The nature of the pain is very important in deciding its cause. A sudden sharp pain is commonly caused by a fissure, or a tear in the lining of the anus that was produced by a hard stool under high force, shearing off anal tissue and exposing one of the many nerves present there. Infections such as herpes simplex can also give similar pain.

An aching, heavy sensation can be caused by a hemorrhoid, an abscess, a solitary rectal ulcer, or a tumor.

Burning and itching can be caused by infections, fissures, hemorrhoids, or even an allergic reaction to the dyes and chemicals in certain toilet tissues.

Intense, cramping, jolt-like pain is called tenesmus, and is associated with inflammation in the rectum as seen in ulcerative colitis, Crohn's disease, and other infections. Thus, it is critical to note carefully the nature of the pain, as it may provide a clue to precise diagnosis and treatment.

ANSWERS TO QUESTIONS ON THE APPEARANCE OF YOUR BOWEL MOVEMENTS

What does it mean when I notice changes in the size and shape of my stool?

Some people would tell you that you are paying too much attention to your b.m.'s and that you are engendering unnecessary things to worry about. This may very well be true, but, if you are having difficulty in passing your stool or are troubled with frequent gas, abdominal pain, or cramps, or have blood or localized rectal pain, then you should observe your stool!

There is much variety in the size and shape of each b.m. The notion that one must pass a tubular, formed, perfectly symmetrical stool everytime has somehow been ingrained into the collective consciousness of a large segment of our society. This is another myth, as it is normal to pass stools that vary in size and shape. If you are experiencing symptoms, then look at the stool in the toilet bowl before flushing and see if there is a consistent thinning of the stool, like a ribbon or a pencil. This means that there is a persistent narrowing of the lower colon or rectum, or excessive pressure in the floor of the pelvis in the muscles that surround the anus.

Most commonly, your symptoms and the associated change in shape of the stool are due to the same factors that produce constipation, excessive gas and bloating, and the sense of incomplete evacuation: inadequate intake of dietary fiber and fluid, and lack of exercise.

Stools that come out as hard marbles or rocks are termed scybalous stools, and are always a result of prolonged delays in the transport of the b.m. through the colon. Diverticulosis of the colon is a common cause of this, especially in the elderly, and is produced by powerful, segmental contractions of the colonic muscles due to a lack of adequate fiber, fluid, and exercise over many decades. These powerful contractions of the colonic muscles impede the passage of the stool and knead it between the contracted segments. When this occurs there is almost always much gas, bloating, and the passage of mucus from the rectum. On extreme occasions an entire pile of these rocks can accumulate in the lower colon, producing an impaction. This is an emergency and must sometimes be relieved by manual or instrumental removal, a most uncomfortable and painful maneuver. When even this is unsuccessful in relieving the impaction, then surgical intervention is required and is attended by a high rate of severe complications.

So, marbles or "rabbit pellets" in the stool are a sign that your diet, fluid, and exercise habits have "sucked" for years, and you had better change them or you'll be in for some scary times!

Of course, there are other factors that can produce such changes in stool size and shape, such as inflammatory conditions and growths. Medications can slow the motility of the bowel and can promote these problems even when you are doing everything right. Drugs such as antihistamines, decongestants, tranquilizers, certain anti-hypertensives, and pain relievers such as narcotics, codeine, and propoxyphene can all lead to constipation and scybalous stools.

Is there a normal stool color?

Not really, as there is considerable variation in the color of the stool, mainly reflecting the color of the food that you have eaten. In our Western diet, the color is usually various shades of brown, resulting from the interaction of our food with digestive juices, bile, and the bacteria residing in the colon.

You should be concerned if your stools turn pitch black and have the consistency of roof tar, a sure sign of blood in the stool most likely from the upper gastrointestinal tract, or the right side of the colon. This stool is also very foul-smelling, emitting a musty, acrid odor that can be detected easily.

Black stools can be the result of eating iron-containing foods, such as leafy dark green veggies like spinach. Iron tablets can also give stool a black color, as can the bismuth in certain medications such as Pepto-Bismol. None of these, however, are sticky and shiny or foul-smelling like those caused by blood. Whenever you see this alarming black stool that we call "melena," you must call your doctor at once, as this is an emergency! If you are dizzy, lightheaded, or are sweating these are signs of major blood loss, and you will need emergency transportation to the nearest emergency room.

Stools that are consistently pale, oily, hard to flush, and extremely horrible smelling contain undigested fat and are reliable signs of malabsorption, a situation produced by a myriad of gastrointestinal disorders that require careful medical investigation.

Other unusually colored stools should not cause concern, such as the orange stool from large amounts of carrots or the dark blue to black stool that occasionally follows the ingestion of excessive amounts of blueberries, blackberries, or boysenberries.

What does it mean if I have blood in my stool, on the toilet tissue, or in the toilet bowl?

Aside from being seen in women during menstruation, it always means that there is something wrong, most usually in the lower colon, rectum, or anus. Most of the time it is due to a fissure in the anus, or "fissure-in-ano," as we like to call it. A fissure is a tear across the lining of the anus, which has a rich blood supply. It is caused by an imbalance between the forces needed to expel the stool, the consistency of the stool, and the resistance in the muscles forming the floor of the pelvis that surrounds the anus. As discussed in other sections of this book, when the stool is too hard and the pelvic muscles are too tense, this imbalance occurs and the weakest link in the chain, so to speak, is the anal lining mucosal cells, which become sheared away, exposing the blood vessels and causing bleeding.

Fissures, although rarely associated with anything serious, **must always be evaluated by a thorough history and examination by your doctor.**

There are many other causes of bloody stools, and none of them are trivial. Hemorrhoids are the next most common cause of blood in the stool. These are large, dilated veins that line the lower rectum and anus. Veins return blood from the tissues to the heart. They have thinner, less elastic walls than the arteries, as they are not designed to experience high pressures as found in the arteries. They are more like slow, even-flowing canals. In fact, the pressure inside them reflects the pressure upstream, toward the heart, or in the case of hemorrhoids, any place upstream such as the surrounding muscles and tissues of the wall of the rectum and colon, and the liver into which they drain. It is reassuring to know that statistically the most common cause of hemorrhoids in our society is not very serious, and is the result of always being in the upright position, aggravated by such common events as pregnancy, a sedentary job such as a truck, bus, or taxi driver, or by repeated straining to have a b.m.

Hemorrhoids can also be caused by increased pressure in the liver due to swelling and/or scarring in the liver cells. Mechanical blockage to the flow of blood from the rectum and anus due to inflammation, scarring, or abnormal growths in the surrounding tissues is very serious and requires careful detailed evaluation by your physician.

Blood in the stool may also be due to growths such as polyps or tumors. There may be bleeding from diverticulosis of the colon, a condition more commonly seen in those over age 65. Vascular abnormalities, due to wear and tear on the colonic wall or to other chronic conditions in the rest of the bowel, can often present as blood in the stool. These latter conditions most often produce sudden, massive bleeds, often free from pain. **ALL OF THESE ARE EMERGENT CONDITIONS AND MUST BE DEALT WITH QUICKLY BY YOUR DOCTOR!**

Other common causes are infectious diarrheas. Although most diarrheas are not serious and are self-limiting, **any diarrhea with blood requires a thorough evaluation by your physician.** Inflammatory bowel disease (Crohn's disease and ulcerative colitis) may present with bleeding and is always considered by your doctor when an evaluation for bloody diarrhea is performed.

Again, blood in the stool is most often not serious but is never trivial, and must always be thoroughly evaluated.

What does it mean when I see mucus in my stool?

Mucus in the stool is a signal of irritation, usually in the lower colon or rectum. Most commonly, it occurs together with constipation, as the hard stool irritates the cells lining the lower colon to produce mucus to act as a lubricant. Mucus also traps offending toxins, organisms, or irritating chemicals, preventing them from gaining access to the body and carrying them out with the stool.

Occasionally, one will pass a small amount of mucus which looks like a clear to pale yellow gelatinous substance. This occasional mucus is of small volume, say, less than half a teaspoon, and is a normal response to the infrequent hard stool. It is when you begin to see mucus with every bowel movement, with somewhat larger volume, that you should be concerned and see your doctor, as this may be a sign that chronic irritation from inflammatory or infectious disease is present. Mucous discharge that occurs by itself, without a b.m., can be a sign of frequent enemas, repeated trauma, or even a tumor. This is a sign of potential trouble and requires expert attention.

I often see undigested food in my stool. Is there something wrong?

There are many foods that cannot be completely digested by the enzymes in your digestive system, but that doesn't mean that you must digest everything you eat. This is a popular myth that pervades the thinking of so many people. Foods such as corn and other vegetables with a skin containing cellulose are not digested by humans because we lack cellulase enzymes. However, such "undigestible" substances perform a very important task - to provide bulk to stretch and tone the muscles of the bowel wall, and thus help produce an easy b.m.

If you are feeling well, maintaining your weight, and have a good appetite you should not be concerned about noticing undigested food in your stool. On the other hand, if you are losing weight and passing frequent loose stools that are foul-smelling and contain undigested food, then it is cause to consult with your physician as soon as you can, as this could be a sign of significant malfunction of your bowel.

Why do my bowel movements burn after I eat very hot or spicy foods?

This is a very common phenomenon, and is likely due to the presence of capsaicin, a chemical found in hot chilies. This compound has fascinating properties related to the stimulation of bowel motility. It also induces painful or pleasantly noxious (depending upon your point of view) nerve impulses from the point of contact in the bowel, while helping transmit them to the spinal cord and the brain.

It is common to have an increase in the frequency of b.m.'s after ingesting foods which contain hot chili peppers, cayenne, or paprika as a significant ingredient. The capsaicin in these spices stimulates contraction of the colon and emptying of the rectum by stimulating components of the nerves that signal the muscles of the colon to contract and relax appropriately. In addition, capsaicin stimulates the release of bowel hormones that increase the secretion of fluid by the small intestine. The peppers thus are more rapidly transported to the rectum and anus, stimulating specialized nerves that let you know that "there's a fire down below!"

However, anyone in New Orleans, the Southwest, Latin America, or Asia can tell you that this burning does not always happen with continued ingestion, as a "desensitization" or tolerance phenomenon occurs with prolonged exposure to capsaicin. There is some evidence that capsaicin in small amounts offers protection to the intestinal and stomach cells that are exposed to it, and that repeated stimulation of pain-transmitting nerves can lessen the sensation of pain. The "bottom" line is that the burning from a spicy meal may be unpleasant or even painful, but it is not likely harmful.

A real exception to this involves those with inflammatory bowel disease such as Crohn's disease and ulcerative colitis, where it has been shown that the nerves responsible in conducting pain information in these conditions are activated by capsaicin. There may also be an increased activation of the inflammation in these conditions, so it is best to avoid hot chilies if you have inflammatory bowel disease.

Is it common to have worms in your stool?

Although worm infestations of the gastrointestinal tract are among the most common infections around the world, they are fortunately much more unusual in developed nations.

Still, poorly-washed vegetables and inadequately cooked or raw meats and fish are the major sources of worms. Food preparers and servers who carry worms and who do not wash their hands carefully after having a bowel movement are common transmitters of worm infections.

Worms can gain entry into your bowel by several routes: some worm larvae can burrow through your bare feet, get into your vascular system and are carried into your lungs where they are coughed up and swallowed into your bowel. Others can have their eggs passed by fecally-contaminated water used to fertilize crops or to feed livestock, and be ingested. Many others can have their eggs live in an intermediate host, such as a water snail, which then develops into larvae which can directly enter your skin or your bowel. Some mature worms can be in the muscles of fish, beef, or pork and can be directly ingested.

With careful food handling and strict attention to hygiene, worms pose little risk in developed nations.

How do I know if I have worms in my stools? Can I see them?

On some occasions, one can see roundworms and certain tapeworms in the stool. On many others, however, the worms can stay in the bowel and only pass their ova or eggs, which are microscopic and therefore invisible.

Most likely, they show up as causes of unexplained weight loss, fatigue, diarrhea, abdominal pain, or anemia. Certain roundworms, such as Ascaris, can proliferate in the upper intestine to such an extent as to cause an obstruction or perforation.

With a careful history and examination of your stools for ova (eggs) and parasites, your physician should be able to diagnose almost every worm infestation and treat it completely.

ANSWERS TO QUESTIONS ON CONSTIPATION

What is constipation?

Constipation occurs when it becomes difficult to pass a stool without straining, and when the stool is much harder in consistency and less frequent than normal.

There usually is variation in stool size, shape, and firmness. So, every once in a while it is not unusual to force out a hard stool. It is when this happens on a consistent basis, say, two to four stools in succession, that constipation becomes a problem.

How long should I go without having a bowel movement before getting concerned that I am constipated?

This depends on your regular bowel habits. In our society, from three movements a day to three a week is considered the range of normal. Many of us labor under the misconception that one must have one movement daily, as if it were inscribed on the marble wall of a religious shrine.

As long as the motions are easy to pass and the stool is soft yet formed, then one shouldn't be worried. If one's usual pattern is to have one to three bowel movements a day then three days without a b.m. should be cause for concern. If one has three motions a week, then not going for five days should be an alert to a possible problem.

Why does pregnancy cause constipation and hemorrhoids?

While constipation and hemorrhoids commonly occur during pregnancy, they certainly are not inevitable.

During pregnancy, the placenta produces hormones that allow the smooth muscles of the uterus and the bowel to relax to accommodate the growing fetus. This has a tendency to slow bowel motility, and thus increases the chance of constipation. However, if you follow the suggestions for bowel health in this book, it is very unlikely that you will experience constipation.

Hemorrhoids are a slightly different story. They are caused by increasing pressure from the growing fetus on the rectal veins, especially in the latter stages of pregnancy. One can minimize this by taking warm tub baths, doing stretching or yoga, and paying attention to such details as not reading on the toilet and not straining during a bowel movement. The good news is that after delivery the hemorrhoids should regress and stay away with a consistent program of good bowel health.

What should I do if I am constipated?

If you need quick relief--that is, within a few hours to a day--then you could try any number of safe, effective laxatives that are readily available over the counter. You must remember that these preparations are **for occasional use only, and repeated use leads to intestinal injury and eventual laxative dependence.**

Milk of magnesia, two tablespoons taken at bedtime, will often produce a bowel movement by the next morning. Senna or cascara leaves (castor oil), or aloe vera one teaspoon, are more rapid-acting and will produce results in four to six hours. Bisacodyl tablets, two in the afternoon, will work earlier than milk of magnesia. Even more rapid relief can be obtained with a bisacodyl suppository or a glycerin suppository, which can work within an hour or so. If one dose of these agents is unsuccessful, then another dose taken the next morning often works and is safe.

If these measures are not working then you should call your doctor, who may prescribe sodium phosphate or magnesium citrate for relief. There is a listing of the most commonly used laxatives and their mechanisms of action following this section.

If you are just slowing down and need more gradual relief, then stool normalizers such as psyllium and cellulose may be helpful. These must be taken every day and should be considered as a dietary fiber, as they pull water into the stool and help to tone the bowel. Psyllium and cellulose do not cause dependence nor do they injure the bowel, but are subject to that good old American philosophy that "if a little bit is good a whole lot more is even better." I have seen many patients who have gone overboard on these agents, getting symptoms of bloating, diarrhea, gas, and cramps. The usual dose of psyllium or cellulose is one rounded tablespoon daily, dissolved in a glass of water or juice and followed by another glass of water.

Many physicians recommend so-called "stool softeners," which are wetting agents that coat the surface of the stool with fluid. I do not recommend them, for in my experience they rarely work.

SUMMARY

- Milk of magnesia, 2 tablespoons at bedtime
- Senna or cascara leaves or aloe vera, one teaspoon
- Bisacodyl, 2 tablets in the afternoon
- Bisacodyl or glycerin suppository, 1 suppository for relief within an hour
- Psyllium or cellulose, 1 rounded tablespoon daily, dissolved in water and followed by a glass of water

What natural or alternative medications are there for the relief of constipation?

I have discussed some of these earlier: senna, cascara, and aloe. These all contain chemicals that irritate the nerves and muscles of the colon, producing contractions and expulsion of the stool. They are safe for occasional use only. The same can be said for yellow dock, an herb commonly found in natural remedies. Prunes, while delicious, also contain the same class of chemical irritants and are not safe for repeated use.

Recently I saw a busy young businesswoman to evaluate her chronic constipation and abdominal pain. She traveled extensively and ate in restaurants and hotels. She exercised and was diligent about her fluid and fiber intake, despite having to eat most of her meals out. She was very much into natural and alternative medication and healing, like so many of my patients. She took prunes every day and a natural herbal laxative that contained senna, aloe, yellow dock, ginger, gingko, licorice, and about twenty other herbs. She had to take more and more of this preparation, until she no longer could have any bowel movements at all unless she took enemas. I colonoscoped her and found the most striking evidence of "laxative abuse colon," or melanosis coli that I have ever seen in my thirty years of practice. The patient thought that just because a remedy was natural it must be safe, and that she could use it with impunity. But, as she learned, this is a misconception.

LAXATIVE PREPARATIONS

Laxatives are organized by their mechanism of action. Those in the first list are the most gentle and are the most physiological, in that they promote the body's own inherent mechanisms to move the stool along in a smooth manner. In the next list are so-called "stool softeners," or wetting agents. They are safe, but in my experience they are of limited value. The third list are contact evacuants, producing reflex contractions of the rectal and colonic muscles. These are very effective when used on an occasional short-term basis. The last group are the neuromuscular irritants, usually of natural origin, and, again, very effective for occasional use. These can lead to dependence when used chronically, producing major injury to the bowel and leading to significant bowel dysfunction.

I have included natural laxatives in each list. Upon reviewing most of the natural preparations available, I have found that most have combinations of many herbs and other natural substances, the interactions of which are not well-characterized. Thus, the lists contain single natural substances organized by their known actions on the bowel. (see p. 36 and p. 37)

LAXATIVE PREPERATIONS

GROUP ONE: BULK FORMERS, "STOOL NORMALIZERS"

Active Ingredient	Brand Name
psyllium oat bran cellulose polycarbophil apple pectin slippery elm guar gum	Metamucil, Serutan, Konsyl, Hydrocil Per Diem, Colon Cleansing Formula, Citrucel, Ultimate Fiber, Ultimate Cleansing, Equalactin

GROUP TWO: STOOL SOFTENERS

Active Ingredient	Brand Name
Docusate	Surfak, Colace, Doxidan

GROUP THREE: CONTACT EVACUANTS

Bisacodyl	Dulcolax, Carter's, Feen-a-Mint, Correctol

GROUP FOUR: NEUROMUSCULAR IRRITANTS

Senna Aloe Yellow Dock Anthroquinones (prunes)	Senokot, Ex-Lax, X-Prep liquid, numerous natural preparations
Cascara	Easy-Lax Plus, Doxidan Plus, Nature's Remedy, numerous natural preparations

GROUP FIVE: NEUROMUSCULAR IRRITANTS AND STIMULATORS OF FLUID SECRETION

Magnesium	Milk of magnesia, Mylanta, Maalox, Chito-San, Magnesium citrate
Sodium Phosphate	Fleet's Phosphosoda

GROUP SIX: NATURAL INGREDIENTS COMMONLY FOUND WITHOUT KNOWN MECHANISMS OF ACTION IN PROMOTING DEFECATION

fenugreek seed	stinging nettle
burdock	Pau D'arco
gentian	black alder
echinacea	honeysuckle
dandelion	yarrow
rhubarb	cinnamon
marshmallow	ginseng
red clover	peppermint oil
ginger	rose hips
goldenseal	hawthorn
wild yam	piper longum
salvia	

GROUP SEVEN: PRESCRIPTION LAXATIVES

Active Ingredient	**Brand Name**
Lactulose syrup	Enulose, Duphalac, Chronulac
sorbitol	
Polyethylene glycol with electrolytes	Golytely, Nu-lytely, Co-lyte, Miralax

Note that phenolphthalein-containing laxatives have been removed from the market, as they have been implicated in causing disease in rodents.

DRUGS KNOWN TO CAUSE CONSTIPATION

Antihistamines, decongestants, cold remedies
any preparation with the following: ephedrine, pseudoephedrine, chlorpheniramine, diphenhydramine

Antidepressants
most of the drugs in this class

Antihypertensives
Clonidine
calcium channel blockers: Verapamil, diltiazem, nifedipine, amlodipine, others

Anti-anxiety agents
benzodiazepines: diazepam, lorazepam, alprazolam

Sleeping pills
benzodiazepines: temazepam, estazolam, triazolam

Anti-Parkinson drugs
Opiates and Pain Relievers
morphine, codeine, meperidine, oxycodone, propoxyphene, tramadol, other opiates

Mineral Supplements
iron, calcium

Antacids
aluminum-containing, sucralfate

Is it ever a good idea to have an enema other than when it is prescribed by a doctor?

No. I know I will be pilloried repeatedly over this, as there are many enemas on the market, readily available, for anyone to use so they must be safe and effective. But, really, if you must use an enema, only do so after you have tried to relieve constipation by the methods discussed in the sections on constipation. If and when you finally use an enema to relieve constipation, and you are unsuccessful, you should consult your physician. You have a significant problem.

There are clinics throughout the United States that give colonic irrigations, but there have been several reports of blowouts of the cecum (the beginning of the colon in the right lower abdomen) due to excessive force and volume of these irrigations or enemas. In addition, incomplete cleansing of the enema device has been widely reported to cause parasitic and other infections of the colon.

If you eat adequate fiber, fresh fruits and vegetables, drink sufficient fluids, and get enough exercise, you are likely never to need an enema. Repeated use of enemas causes injury to the bowel, damaging the muscles and nerves so that you would require more and more enemas every day in order to have any b.m. at all. I'm sure that you have better things to do during the day than to be giving yourself several enemas. I have seen too many patients who have become enema-dependent after starting the seemingly healthful practice of colonic irrigation. Just let nature take its course.

Should I cleanse my bowels by fasting, using coffee enemas, or colon cleansing formulas?

Your bowel already cleanses itself with regular bowel movements, and does not need cleansing by fasting, enemas, or cleansing formulas. The bowel is designed to move its contents from the mouth downward through the anus, and no matter how well intentioned, not to have any substance introduced from the opposite direction. Enemas used to clear the bowel for surgery, x-rays, endoscopy, and other medical purposes are the exception.

Your bowel requires energy from ingested food to maintain its cells, which are constantly being renewed every day. This process safeguards all the functions of the bowel, including protection of the body from invading microorganisms, toxins, and abnormal immune responses. It is in working **with** this design, rather than against it, that you will achieve healthy bowel function.

FASTING

Proponents of fasting believe that it gives overworked cells a rest, and, that by removing food which requires energy for digestion, the body will rid itself of toxins that are present. It is supposed to improve your circulation by "thinning" the blood, thus delivering nutrients more efficiently to the body.

None of these statements are true. The following happens when you fast:

1. Blood sugar levels fall, depriving the brain and nervous system of their main source of energy.
2. The body turns to starch stored in the liver as a short term supply of sugar for the brain.

3. As fasting continues, the body next turns to protein stored in the muscles and bowel to be converted in the liver to sugar.
4. Breakdown products of this protein accumulate and must be excreted by the kidneys, because they are truly toxic to all the body's tissues.
5. Cardiac output falls, causing circulation to become sluggish, accumulating even more toxins.
6. Fasting reduces levels of crucial minerals such as potassium, calcium, and magnesium which produce disturbances in your heart rhythm.
7. Medications can also be affected by fasting.

People who choose to fast for religious purposes should:

1. Check with their physician
2. Fast for no longer than 48 hours
3. Rest
4. Drink at least 8 eight-ounce glasses of water a day
5. After fasting reintroduce foods in small portions

COFFEE ENEMAS

In my practice, I am frequently asked about coffee enemas, especially these days where one can find a specialty coffee house on just about every street corner. I often answer, "Do you want to have it as a latte, cappuccino, or a mocha?" Actually, coffee enemas were popularized about a century ago, derived from the teachings of Dr. Max Gerson. He held that toxins which can cause cancer and produce the pain that accompanies advanced cancer are stored in the liver. In order to rid the body of these toxins, coffee enemas would stimulate the liver to flush them out through the bile.

There are several things wrong with this theory:

1. NO toxin in the bile has been identified that can reproduce cancer or cause pain.
2. There is no evidence that coffee enemas stimulate the liver to secrete bile.
3. Coffee enemas must be given several times a day; doing this can injure the muscles and nerves of the colon.
4. Constipation will result, then you'll <u>really</u> have a problem eliminating toxins.

Better to have your occasional latte or cappuccino at the corner coffee house than have it forced up your rectum several times daily!

COLON CLEANSING FORMULAS

Colon cleansing formulas are a big business in this country. At any health food store or nutrition center you will find shelves stocked with these "miracle" formulas. The problem with these formulations is that they contain mixtures of ingredients (herbs, grains, minerals, and oils) of varying concentrations and purity, many of which have no known effect and several of which have dangerous side effects. The best cleansing program is to allow your bowel to function efficiently, the way nature intended.

ANSWERS TO QUESTIONS ON DIARRHEA

What is diarrhea?

Diarrhea is an increase in the water content of the stool. It is also the passage of frequent loose stools.

Now, everyone passes an occasional loose stool. Even one or two explosive, high volume watery stools can happen on occasion. It is when these loose or watery stools persist beyond one to two days that one must become concerned, and see a doctor. Loose stools that awaken one from sleep are always a sign of a problem that will require medical attention.

When one considers that the intestine is presented with six to eight quarts of fluid every day, and normally only excretes less than a cup of that fluid in the stool, it is amazing that the loose stool occurs only rarely in most people. So, one can easily see that the gastrointestinal tract is very efficient at conserving fluid. Diarrhea occurs when the volume of fluid excreted in the stool exceeds one cup a day.

One can view diarrhea, then, as an imbalance in the bowel's function of producing, absorbing, and conserving fluid. Diarrhea is caused by an overproduction of fluid, a decreased absorption of it, or a combination of both.

Fortunately, many causes of diarrhea go away by themselves, or, to put it more medically, are self-limited. Nonetheless, if you have any diarrhea that lasts more than three days despite proper supportive treatment, or if it has blood in it, then you must be seen and evaluated by a physician as soon as possible.

What do I do if I have diarrhea?

The first thing to realize is that occasional episodes of loose or watery stools are very normal, and not to panic. If you feel well otherwise, without muscle aches, nausea, vomiting, or fever, then you could take two Pepto-Bismol tablets or an Imodium tablet and proceed with your daily life. These unusual bouts of loose stools almost always go away in a day, being cleared by the body's own defenses.

However, if the diarrhea persists beyond a day or two at the most, and is accompanied by any of the above signs, or if it is bloody, then take your temperature, get into bed, and call your doctor. Chances are the physician will tell you to stay in bed, take fluids, and call back if symptoms continue.

Bedrest is a basic method used to slow the activity of the bowels. Indeed, those who do not get enough exercise are often constipated! Bedrest equalizes the pressures throughout the bowels. You should turn frequently and not stay constantly on your back, as this would allow gas and fluid to settle in the middle, upper abdomen, producing pain, nausea, and distention.

Since the fluid excreted in diarrhea is rich in minerals and is derived from the fluid in the bloodstream, it is important to replace the lost volume and minerals. Water alone is inadequate, as lost vital minerals such as sodium and potassium would not be replenished, causing confusion, more muscle aches, and a generally worse overall feeling to occur. So you must use fluids with adequate mineral content. Fortunately, the fluid being produced by the cause of the diarrhea is independent of the process of absorption, so it is easy to replace the lost fluid without worsening the episode. Sodium and potassium are absorbed in the upper small intestine in association with the active absorption of sugars and amino acids. So fluids rich in minerals, sugars, and amino acids are the ideal replacement fluids to use. These are non-caffeinated sodas such as ginger ale, Orangina, and Seven-Up. Sport drinks and Pedialyte are also effective. Clear broths such as vegetable, beef, fish or chicken are excellent. To these, rice or pasta could be added.

There are certain fluids and foods to be avoided when treating diarrhea. Contrary to popular myth, tea should be avoided as it (and coffee and chocolate too) can produce more intestinal fluid loss and stimulate bowel activity.

Dairy products contain lactose, which cannot be digested during the episode (and for several days after the diarrhea has resolved) and worsens the problem by being converted by the normal bacteria in the bowel into organic acids and gas, both of which can produce more diarrhea and discomfort. It is best to just avoid diary products for up to a week after the diarrhea is over. Fats and oils will stimulate the release of gastrointestinal hormones that cause increased fluid production and muscular contractions by the bowel, also making the situation worse. Hot chili peppers will also produce a similar increase in fluid production and motility, so avoid them as well.

At this point, it is best to continue with bedrest and fluid replacement rather than adding an antidiarrheal remedy. The diarrhea actually dilutes and clears the offending agent or toxin that caused the problem in the first place, so anything that would slow this process would likely prolong the diarrhea by allowing extended contact with the intestinal cells. Again, realize that the vast majority of these bouts will run their course in about three days and your symptoms will disappear.

If, on the other hand, the diarrhea is bloody then you should call your doctor immediately, as bloody stools are never trivial and require immediate investigation. If the diarrhea persists after three days of bedrest and fluids, then it must be evaluated by your physician.

SUMMARY

- Pepto-Bismol, 2 tablets or Imodium, 1 tablet
- Bedrest
- Take mineral rich fluids
- Avoid water, tea, dairy products, coffee, fats, and oils
- If you have bloody stools, fever, nausea, vomiting, or muscle aches call your physician

What does it mean if the diarrhea persists after a few days?

Most diarrheal conditions will run their course in three to five days. Diarrhea that continues beyond this time is considered to be persistent.

The most common cause of persistent diarrhea is the irritable bowel syndrome (IBS). This can be characterized by the frequent urge to defecate, irregularity of stool form, the feeling of incomplete evacuation, and abdominal pain relieved by a b.m. Irritable bowel syndrome almost never causes one to awaken from sleep in order to have a b.m. Because of genetic hardwiring, or predisposition, conditioned by emotions and experience, an acute diarrhea will often set off an IBS. A careful history and examination by your doctor can help to establish this diagnosis, and once you realize that this is not a serious condition and learn good dietary, relaxation, and exercise habits your bowel will return to normal over time.

If you have persistent diarrhea your physician should do a series of studies to find a possible cause for the problem. These will include stool examinations for inflammatory cells, cultures for bacteria, and examinations for parasites and protozoa. The stool may also be tested for minerals, fats, and laxatives to uncover the cause. If all of those studies are not informative, then you should be referred to a gastroenterologist. This physician may likely look directly into your colon and sample some of the tissue to be examined for inflammatory bowel disease such as ulcerative colitis, Crohn's disease, microscopic colitis, and collagenous colitis. These latter two diseases can only be diagnosed by biopsy of the lining cells of the entire colon, so a thorough evaluation is necessary. Treatment is available for these disorders, reinforcing the effort made to secure the diagnosis.

If there is weight loss associated with persistent diarrhea, then an investigation of intestinal absorption is mandatory. Malabsorption has many causes, and a discussion of them is far beyond the scope of this book. Suffice it to say that they are an important cause of diarrhea and can be successfully treated once the cause is found.

A very interesting observation about persistent diarrhea was made by Drs. Santa Ana and Fordtran in Houston recently. Their department at the University of Texas School of Medicine is one of the foremost centers for the study and treatment of diarrhea in the world. They studied a very large number of patients sent to them from all over the world with persistent diarrhea who could not be diagnosed by their gastroenterologists or internists. They repeated all of the possible tests that one could perform to diagnose diarrhea. Their tests, too, were unsuccessful in securing a precise diagnosis. They followed these patients very carefully for a year and found that the overwhelming majority of them resolved their diarrhea within a year without any specific treatment. This means that the initial episode of diarrhea triggered abnormal intestinal conservation of fluid that took several months to resolve, but was not associated with any serious disease. This should reassure you that many persistent undiagnosed diarrheas are not serious and will go away by themselves.

What are the most common causes of diarrhea?

Exposure to contaminated food or drink is the most common cause of diarrhea, followed by medication side effects, food intolerances, and the effects of growths and inflammations. The following lists the most common causes of diarrhea:

<u>Overproduction of intestinal secretions:</u>

- Ingestion of pre-formed microbiologic toxins
  - non-typhoidal Salmonella
  - staphylococcus
  - Bacillus cereus
  - Listeria--unpasteurized milk and cheese
  - Clostridia
  - Vibrio disease--cholera, shellfish disease
- Viral disease
- Protozoal disease
  - Giardia
  - Cryptosporidium
- Medication-induced diarrhea
  - antibiotics
  - antacids
  - laxatives
- Dietary intolerance
  - lactase deficiency
  - ingestion of osmotically-active stimulants (artificial sweeteners)
  - excessive xanthines-caffeine, theophylline, chocolate

<u>Overproduction of secretions and decreased colonic conservation:</u>

- Inflammatory conditions
  - invasive bacterial disease
  - E. coli, Shigella, Salmonella, Campylobacter, Yersinia, Vibrio, C. difficile
  - ulcerative colitis
  - Crohn's disease
  - collagenous colitis
  - lymphocytic colitis
- Neoplasms and growths

Alterations in motility and secretion:

- Irritable bowel syndrome
- Malabsorption syndrome

What is travelers' diarrhea, and how do I prevent it?

This form of diarrhea happens when one is exposed to new diets, water supplies, and changes in daily routine when traveling abroad. It is commonly felt that it only happens to North Americans traveling in Latin America or underdeveloped countries. While this is often true, it also happens to anyone traveling abroad, even those who come to North America from other countries.

The causes are numerous, but usually different strains of the usual intestinal bacteria are the most common cause. Sometimes parasites such as protozoa are implicated, and, rarely, worms. The diarrhea is mostly produced by a toxin that is found in these bacteria that causes the intestine to secrete fluid. On rare occasions, there is direct invasion of the intestinal lining cells by the bacteria, protozoa, or worms.

Of course, one should be circumspect in consuming foods washed with water, and be careful of salads, especially in Asia where human excrement can be used for fertilizer. I just saw a prominent businessman who stayed at a five-star hotel in Vietnam, who developed a terrible case of disabling diarrhea after eating a salad at this hotel. All of those in his party also fell victim to the lettuce fertilized by human feces!

In general, drink bottled beverages and be sure that your food is well-cooked. Be wary of buffets that have creamed dishes or creamed or custard desserts that have been partially rewarmed, especially if they have been outdoors in the sun.

These are great culture media for bacteria that cause food poisoning, such as Staphylococci and Salmonella.

Many physicians recommend antibiotics to take while you are in the new environment, and there are good studies to support their use. However, since the causes of travelers' diarrhea are diverse, these antibiotics cannot possibly cover all the possible culprits. Instead, it is best to take a medication that interferes with most of the probable mechanisms that produce the diarrhea: attachment of the offending organism to the intestinal cells, neutralization of toxins produced by the organisms within the intestinal lumen, and a reduction of fluid produced by the bowel in response to the organisms. That medication is Pepto-Bismol.

Take two tablets or two teaspoons of the Pepto-Bismol between each meal for the first day in the new country, then one tablet or one teaspoon between meals each day for the next three days. One tablet or one teaspoon should be taken daily for the duration of your trip. I recall the trip that a patient of mine made to China in the 1970's with a large delegation from the Red Cross. I advised her to take Pepto-Bismol, while the others in her party used antibiotics. They visited most of China, and many in the party had severe diarrhea, some of whom had to be air-evacuated to Beijing and Hong Kong for treatment, while my patient never had one day of discomfort.

SUMMARY

- Drink bottled beverages
- Beware of uncooked foods
- Outdoor buffet creamed dishes should be avoided
- Pepto-Bismol
  Two tablets or two teaspoons between meals for the first day
  One table or one teaspoon between meals for the next three days.
  One tablet or one teaspoon daily for the duration of trip

MEDICATIONS FOR DIARRHEA

There are a limited number of effective and safe medications to use for diarrhea. This contrasts with the very large and often confusing number of preparations available for constipation.

Remember, in the acute situation, diarrhea is a mechanism the body uses to flush away the offending organism or toxin that caused the diarrhea in the first place. So, use these preparations in the acute setting until you are able to get into bed and replace the lost fluids appropriately.

These medications are grouped in the order of my preference for treating and preventing diarrhea.

MEDICATIONS THAT PREVENT BACTERIAL ATTACHMENT TO INTESTINAL CELLS

Pepto-Bismol

MEDICATIONS THAT NEUTRALIZE BACTERIAL AND OTHER TOXINS IN THE LUMEN OF THE BOWEL

Pepto-Bismol

cholestyramine resin (available only by prescription)

MEDICATIONS THAT REDUCE FLUID SECRETION BY THE BOWEL

Pepto-Bismol
Imodium
Lomotil

MEDICATIONS THAT SLOW BOWEL MOTILITY

Imodium
Lomotil

PRESCRIPTION DRUGS FOR DIARRHEA

prescription strength Imodium
prescription strength Lomotil
codeine phosphate
tincture of opium
tincture of belladonna
cholestyramine resin

DRUGS CAUSING DIARRHEA

Most of these medications produce diarrhea most commonly as a side effect in elderly patients. In most everyone else, drug-induced diarrhea is very rare as opposed to drug-induced constipation. The list that follows includes only a broad classification.

prostaglandins
parasympathetic mimetic agents (bethanechol)
cardiovascular agents (quinidine)
cancer chemotherapeutic agents
antibiotics
Colchicine
magnesium-containing antacids

medications suspended in sorbitol
enteral food supplements (usually in hospitalized, ill patients)

ANSWERS TO QUESTIONS ON GAS

Which foods cause the most gas, and which ones cause the gas to smell?

Another profound question for the ages! Everyone knows that beans produce gas, but actually the production of gas by the gastrointestinal tract depends on more than just the intake of food. It also depends upon the transit of the food and its absorption by the bowel, and the interaction of any non-absorbed food with microorganisms present in the colon.

Carbohydrates are the most common source of gas. Lactose, the carbohydrate in dairy products and many food additives, is the most common gas producer in those people who are deficient in lactase enzyme.

The Top 5 Carbohydrate Gas Producers

1. Beans, legumes
2. Cooled cooked potatoes
3. Bread
4. Cornflakes
5. Partly milled seeds and grains (cracked wheat, barley, psyllium)

Some of these undigested carbohydrates will be converted into short chain fatty acids, which are the major energy source for the colonic cells, so it is important that some of the food you ingest escapes digestion and absorption. Other carbohydrates on this list provide bulk for normal stools, so do not avoid eating them just because they are on the list.

Although the vast majority of the volume of gas produced is derived from carbohydrate, it is the fermentation of undigested amino acids from protein that imparts the worst odors. Some proteins have sulfur-containing amino acids. These are broken down by the colonic bacteria into hydrogen sulfide and sulfur dioxide, imparting the deadly rotten egg smell that can really disgust one.

Fats that have not been absorbed, when accompanied by poorly-absorbed amino acids and carbohydrates, produce the world's most malodorous stools and are indicative of a severe absorption problem that requires immediate medical attention. It is not necessary to list all the proteins and fats responsible for malodorous gas because that list would encompass almost every food that we eat!

That brings us to the universal truth about intestinal gas: In carefully conducted studies, it has been shown that people who complain about producing a lot of gas do not make more gas than those who do not have such complaints. Rather, these "gas factories" are trapping intestinal gas between segments of contracted bowel due to irregular and powerful contractions of their intestinal muscles. These muscles are poorly toned because of bad dietary habits and inadequate exercise and fluid intake.

Thus, the guidelines discussed in other sections of this book will help you avoid embarrassing emissions and reduce air pollution for all of us!

Sometimes when I pass gas it is embarrassingly loud, and at other times there is no noise at all. Why is this so?

This results from the volume of gas, the force required for its expulsion, and the resistance it must overcome.

This is like letting air out of a balloon. If there is a lot of air and you stretch the opening of the balloon so that it is narrow and tight, the expelled air will produce a loud noise. On the other hand, if you keep the opening of the balloon loose and wide there will be only a little or low-pitched sound emitted.

When there is tension in the wall of the lower colon and rectum, as well as in the floor of the pelvis surrounding the anus, any gas that is passed under these conditions will make noise. By contrast, it is well known that one passes gas while asleep, but it is hardly ever heard because the bowel and the muscles of the pelvic floor are relaxed while you sleep.

There have been some fascinating examples of this phenomenon from the last century, when entertainment took place in such famed music halls in Europe as the Moulin Rouge in Paris. There, the career of one artist, Joseph Pujol, reached its peak when M. Pujol was able to imbibe large volumes of air into his rectum, and, by controlling the tension in his abdominal and anal muscles, he was able to expel it in the form of animal noises, tunes, and other auditory (and, hopefully, not olfactory) emissions! It is said that he was such a "hot" item that he outdrew some of the day's leading stars, such as the esteemed actress Sarah Bernhardt!

All of this erudite dissertation brings me to quote a dirty limerick that I acquired through that great cultural cauldron known as high school:

A daring young man from Sparta
Was widely renowned as a farter
He could fart anything
From "Of Thee I Sing"
To Beethoven's Moonlight Sonata!

I often feel the need to pass gas but can't. Why?

The urge to pass gas (or stool, for that matter) is caused by an increase in the tension of the wall of the rectum. Normally, this will signal the nerves in the spinal cord to send out a series of coordinated messages to the muscles of the floor of the pelvis to contract and open the anus, as well as to the muscles of the colon and rectum to contract and relax appropriately and allow passage of gas.

When you cannot pass gas in response to the urge, it means that there is excessive tension in the muscles that support the rectum in the floor of the pelvis, as well as in the wall of the rectum and colon itself. The causes of this problem are exactly the same as those that cause constipation and the sense of incomplete evacuation of the stool. The treatment is also the same--relax and enjoy your food, don't hurry, take in enough fluid, fiber, fresh fruits and vegetables, get adequate exercise, and sit properly on the toilet seat.

Why do I always have so much gas when I awaken in the morning?

You should know that **everyone** has gas in the morning, and, indeed, everyone passes small amounts of gas during the night while they are asleep. So if you hail the morning, so to speak, by sounding the "greeting trombone," you do not necessarily have a problem.

When you lie down in bed you are horizontal and lying flat, or flatter than you were during the day. The external atmospheric pressure becomes equalized across your abdomen. During the night, the motility of your bowel slows, allowing for an accumulation of gas. When you arise in the morning there is an increase in motility and upper intestinal pressure, forcing gas into the rectum, distending it, and creating the urge to expel the gas.

So it is not unusual to pass gas in the morning; it's when you pass frequent, large, and malodorous salvos that you have to worry about possible medical problems. These problems reflect disturbances caused by abnormal bowel motility, poor absorption of food, taking various medications, hormonal disturbances, and primary structural alterations in the bowel wall produced by disease.

For such frequent "wretched excesses," you must see your physician, who can begin to explore the possibilities with you.

FOODS COMMONLY ASSOCIATED WITH GAS PRODUCTION

Bengal gram dal
peanuts
dried soya beans
dried red lentils
dried green lentils
dried kidney beans
butter beans
fried chick peas
haricot beans (white, dried)
cabbage, raw
pinto beans
garden peas
kidney beans, canned
baked beans, canned
cabbage, cooked
green lentils, canned

* Many gas-producing carbohydrates from dried beans can be eliminated by soaking the beans overnight in water and discarding the water before cooking.

MEDICATIONS TO REDUCE GAS

Most of these medications may produce temporary relief of flatulence, and, in my experience, have little long term effects since they address only the symptoms rather than the cause of gas.

Medications reducing volume of produced gas
- simethicone (Phazyme, Gas-X, Mylicon)
- activated charcoal

Medications reducing gas-forming carbohydrates
- enzymes-alpha galactosidase
  - Beano
  - Yes to Beans
  - Pre-Vail

These latter two products also contain many other enzymes and herbs that have no known action in reducing gas.

ANSWERS TO QUESTIONS ON COLONOSCOPY AND FLEXIBLE SIGMOIDOSCOPY

What are colonoscopy and flexible sigmoidoscaopy?

To diagnose and treat diseases of the colon and to prevent colorectal cancer, your physician may recommend these procedures. They are diagnostic and therapeutic procedures that allow a physician to observe the lining of the entire colon (colonoscopy) or the lower left side of the colon (sigmoidoscopy). These procedures are performed using highly advanced, flexible instruments that are actually video cameras which give a sharp and detailed view of the colon to the endoscopist. Flexible sigmoidoscopy is often performed in the physician's or surgeon's office. It is a limited examination that only takes a few minutes and does not usually require sedation. This procedure allows the endoscopist to diagnose lower colonic problems, take biopsies, or remove polyps. It is of little use, however, as a screening test for colorectal cancer, because less than half of the colon can be visualized with this examination.

Colonoscopy examines the entire colon. It is performed by gastroenterologists and colorectal surgeons who have had extensive training in this technique. Colonoscopy is done in a hospital's ambulatory surgery center. Sedation is required and the procedure takes an experienced endoscopist about fifteen to twenty minutes to complete. This procedure is used for colorectal cancer screening and for removing polyps as well as for obtaining biopsies of masses or growths. Biopsies of the lining cells of the colon are often taken to help diagnose difficult cases of diarrhea and disordered bowel function.

On the day prior to either of these examinations the patient is given a colon cleansing solution to drink, and placed on a clear liquid diet that will allow for full visualization of the colon.

These tests have provided major breakthroughs in the diagnosis and treatment of colonic disorders.

Could I have the fecal ocruit blood test (FOBT) instead of a colonoscopy to screen for colon cancer?

You could, but you shouldn't. While the FOBT can detect a silent colon cancer (one that does not produce any symptoms), and has been shown to lower the death rate from colon cancer by almost 20%, it can often miss polyps and cancers that are not shedding red blood cells at the time of testing. To be most effective you should have a FOBT at least every six months, and you must be on a specialized diet and avoid many medications for three days before testing, as many foods and medications can produce a false positive result. All positive results must be followed by colonoscopy, while negative results can miss polyps and cancers.

The difference between FOBT and colonoscopy is an important one: FOBT can find a cancer before it causes symptoms, while a colonoscopy can find a polyp before it becomes a cancer. To treat a cancer one must have surgery at the least, with possible additional radiation and chemotherapy, while a colonoscopy can safely remove a polyp within minutes, avoiding any possibility of cancer.

Colonoscopy, according to guidelines in this book, has been repeatedly demonstrated to be the most effective and economic means for screening colon cancer.

ANSWERS TO QUESTIONS ON THE EFFECTS OF BOWEL MOVEMENTS ON YOUR HEALTH

Can having good bowel function reduce my risk for heart disease?

Most definitely. So many of the factors that insure excellent bowel function also serve to lower your risk for coronary artery disease. Dietary factors, exercise, and adequate fluid intake have been discussed at length in other sections of this book with regard to bowel function. Relaxing, deep breathing, and taking the time to enjoy life's simple pleasures such as eating a delicious, healthy meal are also crucial to normal bowel actions, as well as reducing the risk from heart disease.

Exercise not only tones the bowel but also lowers blood pressure, reducing injury to the coronary arteries as well as making the heart beat more efficiently. The proper amount of fat in your diet will stimulate the hormones that help to provide optimal bowel motility, but will also stimulate the flow of bile from the liver. The bile will help to absorb the fat and add the proper water content to the stool. Since bile acids are made in the liver from cholesterol, cholesterol is taken out of the bloodstream and the walls of the arteries under these conditions.

Eating adequate fiber from grains, fruits, and vegetables will bind bile acids and cholesterol in the bowel, calling forth even more bile to be produced in the liver from circulating cholesterol. So the stools are formed optimally, the bowel is toned, and cholesterol is lowered even further. I think there is hardly any better example of the interaction of the bowel with the rest of the body than this relationship. The feedback is often instantaneous--as you are promoting healthy bowel function you can almost feel the benefits on your heart!

How can normal bowel function reduce my risk for cancer?

Insuring normal bowel function by the methods outlined in this book will reduce your risk for not only bowel cancer but for many other cancers as well.

Having regular bowel movements limits the contact time of many potential cancer-causing toxins and foodstuffs with the lining cells of the gastrointestinal tract. This reduces the chances for these agents to interact with the genetic controls of cell division, limiting the activation of cancer-causing mutations.

Furthermore, eating adequate amounts of fresh fruits and vegetables insures good muscle tone of the bowel and promotes normal motility, and also provides protective factors against cancer. It is debated whether some of these factors might include beta carotene, but it is clear that brightly-colored fruits and vegetables offer protection.

Can having good bowel movements control my weight?

Yes. Since there is more material written, published, and hyped about diet and weight loss than just about any other subject in our culture, perhaps I should just leave it at the one-word answer, "yes." However, it is precisely because of overdone fad and ill-conceived dietary advice that a rational yet simple and fundamentally sound approach linking good bowel function to weight control is really needed.

We should realize a basic physiologic principle at the outset of this discussion: in the typical adult there is a balance between the amount of nutrition, or food, that is consumed and the amount that is utilized for energy and for the repair and growth of all the cells and tissues of the body. In most people, body weight is commonly maintained within a range of a few pounds over most of their lives. The sensible approach to weight, then, dictates that to lose weight one should increase energy expenditure or diminish caloric intake, or do both.

The factors in our Western society that promote the prevalence of obesity are the same ones that foster difficulty with bowel problems, and disturb this balance. These factors are lack of meaningful exercise, a diet high in fats and low in fresh fruits, vegetables, and grains, an inadequate intake of fluid, and the inability to relax, get away, and just do nothing if only for a few minutes every day.

Exercise tones the bowel muscles and nerves, insuring normal b.m.'s; exercise also burns calories. So many of us are sedentary most of our days, on our jobs, during commuting, or while at home. We mistakenly think that the activity of walking or standing provides enough exercise. While this is better than being completely chairbound, it simply isn't adequate. Almost every patient that I see for constipation, gas, and irritable bowel syndrome lacks enough vigorous exercise in their daily routine. Increasing aerobic exercise on a regular basis also increases the efficiency of metabolism such that calories are burned rather than stored.

As alluded to earlier, such lack of activity also slows bowel action and leads to gas, bloating, constipation, and many other problems. A brisk walk at least three times a week for twenty to thirty minutes is the minimum one needs for basic aerobic fitness. If one forsakes the elevator and takes the stairs for a flight or two during work each day, a few more calories will be burned and the bowel will be toned as well.

Getting more vigorous exercise will, of course, help you to lose some weight and tone your bowel even more. But there is a limit to the amount of exercise that is safe for your bowel. The medical literature is replete with examples of severe problems related to overdoing exercise: gastrointestinal bleeding, disordered emptying of the stomach, and reflux esophagitis are just a few of these problems. These problems usually occur when compulsive exercise is used to excessively reduce weight and is often intricately linked to eating disorders.

So, the connection between body weight and bowel function and exercise is intimate, and should be kept at a reasonable level.

A good rule to remember is to take in most of your calories when your body needs them; that is, at the times when you are active. So many patients that I see with weight problems may not be consuming that many extra calories, but they are taking in the vast majority of their food at dinner and going to bed shortly thereafter. They try to compensate for this during the day by skipping either breakfast or lunch, but by the time dinner rolls around they are famished. It would be much better to consume a moderate breakfast that includes fresh fruits and grains, have a good lunch including at least one or two vegetables and a piece of fruit, and have a much smaller dinner. Do this, and your weight will not be such a problem and your bowels will also function more smoothly.

Keeping fat intake to a reasonable level will help control your weight, and will provide just the right balance of bowel hormone secretion to keep your bowel moving smoothly without excessive cramping or gas trapping. A modicum of fat will stimulate bile secretion by the liver, which will add just the right amount of fluid to the bowel movement, as well as lowering cholesterol. Around twenty percent of the total day's caloric intake should accomplish these functions.

Carbohydrate intake has recently come into focus as a key factor in weight control, and has been featured in so-called "rotation" diets. We have referred to carbohydrates earlier as the most significant source of intestinal gas. This food group probably has the least effect upon bowel function, except for its gas-producing properties. Restricting carbohydrates will doubtless help to lose weight, and perhaps reduce a little gas as well. However, the protective effects of fresh fruits and vegetables will be lost if you reduce too much carbohydrate in your diet. Having five servings of fresh fruits and vegetables every day will not overload you with carbohydrates, especially if you emphasize vegetables, as they are rich sources of protein, minerals, and soluble fiber.

The other important component of providing normal bowel function is fluid intake. Eight glasses of fluid daily will ensure the optimal consistency to your stool, and will serve to fill your stomach a little and may have some effect on reducing the volume of food that you consume. If you use water rather than soda as your fluid choices, then you'll further reduce your caloric intake.

Do I really lose weight after a b.m.? Why do I feel like I have lost weight after defecation?

You actually **do** lose weight--the weight of the actual stool itself. Once the rectum has emptied itself, the diminution in wall tension changes the frequency of signals from the nerves in the rectal wall to the spinal cord and to the brain, where they are processed, telling you that you are now comfortable.

However, you do **not** lose body fat or muscle, just the weight of the stool. So trying to lose weight by purging yourself of stool will not accomplish anything but damage to your bowel, as well as confounding the signals sent to the brain.

Do eating disorders--anorexia nervosa and bulimia--interfere with having normal bowel movements?

Absolutely. Since these problems are associated with the very intake and elimination of food, it stands to reason that they would have a profound effect upon bowel function.

Anorectics restrict their food intake for a number of complex reasons. Since fuel and fiber are being restricted there is little to stimulate bowel function, and constipation is a very common problem among these people. In my practice I have seen many such patients who go for as long as ten to fourteen days before having a bowel movement that is very hard, pellet-like, and difficult to pass. There is mucus often passed with these "rabbit stools," and sporadic rectal bleeding from anal fissures is not uncommon.

Anorectics have many other problems that affect their b.m.'s. The ability of the stomach to empty properly is impaired, again from the very lack of food to stimulate it, as well as from abnormal signals from the brain that reinforce this problem. In addition, since very little fat leaves the stomach, there is virtually no stimulus for bile secretion from the liver, and cholesterol elimination from the bloodstream is reduced, leading to high cholesterol levels along with hard stools.

Anorectics are constipated even more due to the intense tension in their pelvic floor muscles, most likely as a result of the complex emotional factors at work in their disease. This produces resistance to passing the stool.

Bulimics have even more problems. Like anorectics, bulimics who induce vomiting deliver very little food and fuel to the lower bowel, and can be similarly constipated. In addition, the act of repeated vomiting produces intense spasm of the muscles of the stomach and upper small intestine, interrupting the smooth flow of nervous, hormonal, and muscular function that help to produce a normal bowel movement.

Bulimics who binge and then vomit accentuate the confusion of these carefully integrated functions even more, as signals of fullness are intermixed with those of rapid stomach emptying, producing a jumble of traffic between the bowel and the brain, causing bloating, cramping, and rectal urgency.

Even worse, bulimics who use laxatives to purge themselves of stool, thinking that this will control their weight, commonly have terrible problems with constipation, as the repeated use of laxatives injure the nerves and muscles of the bowel, leading to the need to use even more laxatives which establishes a vicious cycle. I have seen a number of these patients who eventually lose control over their anal and rectal function, enhancing an already profound emotional depression and diminished sense of self esteem.

There are many more adverse effects of these eating disorders on bowel function, but a discussion of them is far beyond the scope of this book. However, even this brief discussion should allow one to gain sound insight on the profound interaction of the emotions and the bowel.

How does anal sex affect my bowel movements?

The expulsion of the stool requires a carefully coordinated and sequenced series of events that depend upon an intact functioning rectum and anus. Any repeated instrumentation of this area by any invasive device can be associated with damage to the nerves and muscles that are crucial to this function. In addition, the introduction of the agents of sexually-transmitted diseases can produce inflammation and tissue destruction that can lead to painful defecation, mucous discharge, and loss of control of the anal sphincter.

The most common problems associated with frequent anal invasion are an inability of the rectal nerves to adequately sense the presence of stool. This can lead to overflow incontinence and inability to retain the b.m. so that it can be released at socially more opportune times. Repeated damage to this area can also lead to stenosis or narrowing of the anal canal, which can cause one to repeatedly strain to have a b.m. This in turn can produce stretching of the pudendal nerve, the main nerve that controls the anal sphincter and can cause further inability to control defecation.

I have diabetes, how does it affect my bowel function?

Diabetes affects the blood supply and nervous control of the bowel. The expression of diabetes varies so much from person to person, a wide range of disordered functions can occur. There are many, if not most, diabetics who do not experience any bowel or digestive symptoms; others, however, can have severe bloating from delayed emptying of their stomach, diarrhea from poor clearance of bacteria from the small intestine, or the inability to sense the urge to defecate and suffer loss of fecal control.

Each problem needs to be explored individually with your physician, so that the mechanism of the problem can be elucidated, allowing for specific treatment. What is clear, however, is that close attention to the dietary, fluid and exercise recommendations in this book will help to control the blood sugar and help to minimize the complications of diabetes on the bowel.

How would lactose intolerance affect my bowel movements?

If you are lactose intolerant you will likely experience diarrhea, bloating, gas, and abdominal pain after consuming dairy products in large amounts. This occurs when milk sugar (lactose) is ingested in the presence of too little intestinal enzyme (lactase) to be digested. The undigested lactose is then fermented into gas and irritating organic acids by the bacteria in the colon, producing these problems.

There are easy ways to avoid the problems of lactose intolerance and still obtain the benefits of the excellent nutrition found in dairy products. When consuming dairy products do it slowly, and in small quantities with other food. This will cause the stomach to deliver tiny amounts of lactose that can be easily handled even in the most lactose intolerant person. There are many products available that are designed specifically for this problem. Lact-Aid drops and tablets that are taken before meals, and yogurt, kefir, or acidophilus milk, which contain bacterial cultures that pre-digest the lactose for you.

How does aging affect my bowels?

As we age there is a slowing of esophageal motility, decrease in stomach acid, reduction of fluid production by the small intestine, and slowing of colonic motility. This has resulted in over a billion dollars a year in laxative sales, primarily to the elderly!

Although this may sound depressing there is a light at the end of this tunnel, and it's not from a colonoscope, either! If you follow the principles outlined in this book which emphasize exercise, fluid intake, relaxation, and diet, then much of the decline in bowel function can be avoided.

As we age it is even more important to consume adequate fluids, due to the diminished production of intestinal fluid. Since arthritis of the spine, hips, and knees limits the ability to sit properly on the throne, it is important to stretch and exercise each day. Another common problem that limits the intake of fiber, and thus impairs smooth defection, is ill-fitting dentures and the inability to chew solids properly. Efforts should be made to puree foods and see your dentist, so that the wonderful benefits of food can be enjoyed. Many medications taken by the older patient can also be a factor, so check with your physician to be sure that the recommendations made here are compatible with your health status.

With attention to these details, one can minimize the decline of bowel function that occurs with aging, and enjoy many years of good health and productivity.

What is the irritable bowel syndrome?

The irritable bowel syndrome (IBS) is a group of complex symptoms that together are characteristic of a disorder of the gastrointestinal system. These symptoms are:

- various degrees of abdominal pain
- gas
- bloating
- changes in the frequency and consistency of bowel movements
- sense of incomplete evacuation of stool

IBS is extremely common and is caused by abnormalities in the intricate relationship between the mind and the bowel. These make one exquisitely aware of normal bowel activities that would otherwise go unnoticed in those without IBS. They can make a pleasant sensation—such as the comfortable feeling of fullness after a meal—seem painful. While not life-threatening, such symptoms are extremely disabling. Many of the questions in this book actually address aspects of IBS, but a full exploration of this common disabling condition is best undertaken with a gastroenterologist along with your primary care physician.

CHAPTER IV

COLORECTAL CANCER (COLON CANCER)

CHAPTER IV
COLORECTAL CANCER (COLON CANCER)

COLORECTAL CANCER (COLON CANCER)

Colorectal cancer is now the second leading cause of cancer deaths in the United States, with the average person having a 1 in 16 chance of developing this disease in their lifetime. With these frightening statistics it is important for everyone to understand its causes and means of prevention.

In the last thirty years, our knowledge of how to treat and prevent this disease has changed dramatically. When I was a medical student, the early detection and prevention of this cancer was not possible, and when diagnosed, it was usually too late for treatment. Those patients that could be treated were given surgery in hope of removing the cancer, but this method often proved unsuccessful.

Years of scientific research have revealed that colon cancer develops as a result of the interaction between genetic and environmental factors. We know that colon cells are programmed by our genes to grow, mature, and die rapidly, so that the lining of the colon is completely replaced every 36 to 48 hours. These colon cells, however, can become cancerous as the result of changes or mutations in the genes promoted by environmental factors, such as diet, alcohol, tobacco smoke, pollutants, medications, and the stresses of life.

More than 90 percent of all colorectal cancers begin as polyps (Fig. 3). Polyps are clusters of cells lining the colon that grow more rapidly and die less quickly than their neighboring cells as a result of genetic mutations. In this early stage of their

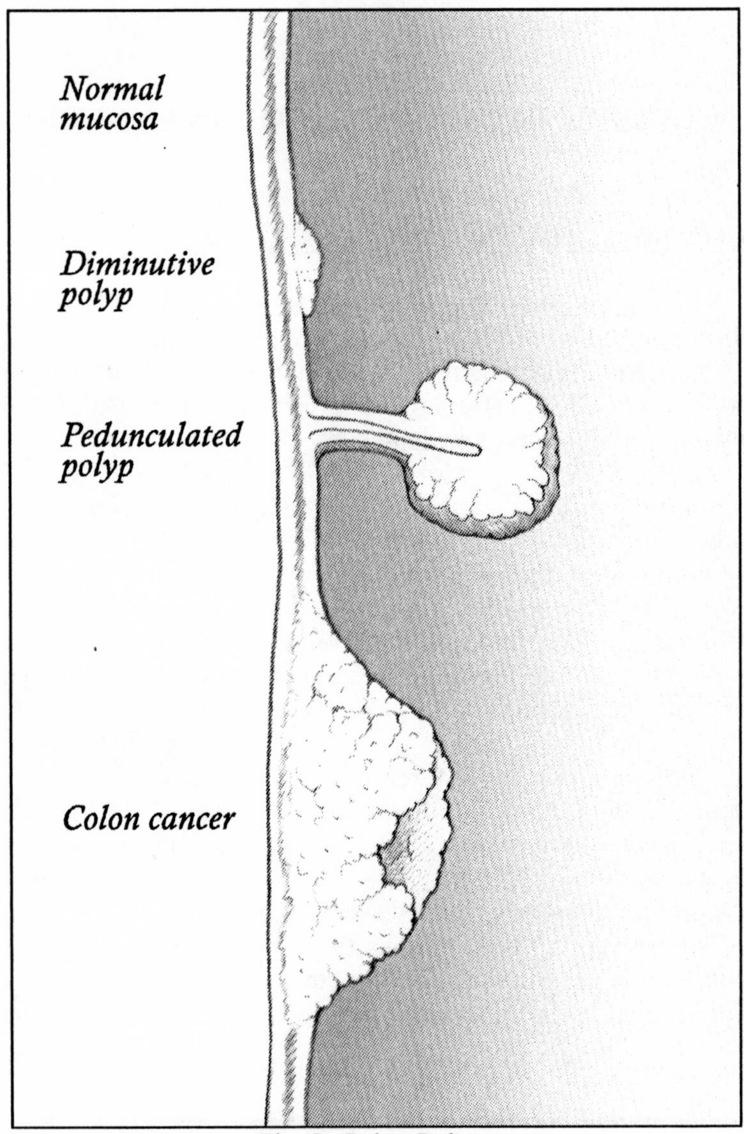

Fig. 2 Colon Polyps

development, when they are less than 2 cm in size, the polyps rarely cause symptoms and are not cancerous; however, over a period of three to seven years they can grow larger, undergo further mutations, and become cancerous with symptoms of bleeding, anemia, and changes in bowel habits.

This is why identifying and removing polyps before they produce symptoms is so crucial. Today, the most effective way of early detection and removal is colonoscopy. It is a procedure performed by trained gastroenterologists and colorectal surgeons, using a highly advanced, flexible instrument (colonoscope) which is a video camera that gives a sharp and detailed view of the colon.

After the polyps have been identified, they are removed by various instruments that are passed through the colonoscope, and examined by a pathologist who determines if cancer cells are present and if they have invaded the base or stalk of the polyp. If a cancer is detected but confined to only the polyp, the cancer is considered completely cured when the polyp has been removed. However, if the base or stalk of the polyp has been invaded, then that area of the colon and its adjacent lymph nodes must be surgically removed. The surgically removed sections are then examined by the pathologist to determine if cancer cells have invaded the wall of the colon or the body's circulation.

If no invasion has been detected then no further treatment is required, but colonoscopy must be done annually to survey and remove any new polyps that might develop. If a gross cancer is present, treatment after surgery depends on the type and extent of the cancer removed. Options such as chemotherapy, radiation, and laser surgery should be discussed with your gastroenterologist and oncologist, with a follow-up colonoscopy performed within a year.

Many patients are fearful that they may have to wear a colostomy bag after colon cancer surgery, but for most patients this is not required. It only becomes necessary when the tumor is very large and found lying very low in the rectum.

This procedure of detecting and removing polyps early has helped to lower the mortality rate for colorectal cancer substantially, and has benefited millions of people. The following are the recommended guidelines for the use of colonoscopy in screening for colorectal cancer:

(see table on next page)

If you are of

AVERAGE RISK (No family history of colorectal, uterine, ovarian, pancreatic, kidney, or breast cancer):

- Colonoscopy at age 50
- Repeat in 10 years if normal
- Repeat in 3 years if polyps are found and removed

If there is

COLORECTAL CANCER IN ONE OR TWO FIRST DEGREE RELATIVES (PARENT OR SIBLING) LESS THAN 60 YEARS OLD:

- Colonoscopy at age 40
- Repeat in 10 years if normal
- Repeat in 3 years if polyps are found and removed

If there is a

FAMILY HISTORY OF MULTIPLE POLYPS, OR SKIN CYSTS, OR SPOTTY PIGMENTATION OF THE LIPS OR EARLY IRREGULAR BALDNESS TOGETHER WITH SKIN CANCERS:

- Colonoscopy starting at puberty

If you have

INFLAMMATORY BOWEL DISEASE (ULCERATIVE COLITIS AND CROHN'S DISEASE):

- Surveillance colonoscopy every 1-3 years, depending on the course of the disease

The prevention of the development of colon cancer is equally important. In the early 1970's, revolutionary research demonstrated a connection between bowel movements and colorectal cancer. One of the vanguard studies was done by Dr. Dennis Burkitt, an epidemiologist from the University of London. In his research, Dr. Burkitt compared the dietary habits of people in developed and underdeveloped countries, and concluded that people who ate a diet high in plant fiber and had regular, large bowel movements had a much lower incidence of colon cancer.

For the first time, a relationship between diet, bowel movements, and cancer had been established. At the same time, important studies by Drs. Drasar, Armstrong, and Doll from Oxford, England, and Dr. Jeremiah Stamler from the Mayo Clinic concluded that a high fat diet increased the risk for colon cancer. These studies and many others demonstrate the importance of reducing fat and increasing fiber in the diet.

The Harvard University School of Public Health has provided even more evidence for preventing colorectal cancer. For over 20 years they have been conducting studies involving thousands of doctors and nurses, and found that multiple vitamins—especially folic acid—when taken every day can lower our risk for colon cancer by 15 percent in 5 years and 74 percent in 15 years. They have also confirmed that calcium supplementation and aspirin reduce the development of polyps.

Vitamin E, fish oils, and brightly colored fruits and vegetables have also been shown to prevent polyps and colorectal cancers. Emotional stress and inactivity have been linked to the disease. The following are the recommended guidelines for lowering the risk of colorectal cancer.

- Regular checkups with your physician
- Colonoscopy at appropriate time intervals
- Do not smoke, and avoid secondhand smoke
- Moderate alcohol intake
- Limit heavily charbroiled foods
- Avoid animal fats
- Eat a diet rich in whole grains, fruits, and vegetables
- Drink adequate fluids
- Get regular exercise
- Relax

Take the following supplements:

- 1 multivitamin daily
- Vitamin E 1000 units daily
- Vitamin C 500 mg daily
- Calcium 1000-1200 mg daily
- Folic acid 400 mcg (may be in multivitamins) daily
- Fish oil 4000 mg daily
- 1/4 strength aspirin, 3 times/week

CHAPTER V

THE BOWEL HEALTH AND COLON CANCER PREVENTION PLAN

CHAPTER V

THE BOWEL HEALTH AND COLON CANCER PREVENTION PLAN

DIET

This diet is about the joy and pleasure of eating. It's about a love of life, a love of health, and most of all, a love of self that should last an entire lifetime. This diet is about pleasure, not punishment; it will be an addition rather than a restriction to your life. And, as this diet works in harmony with the other parts of our plan, you should notice in 10 to 14 days a significant improvement in your bowel function, a signal that you are on the way to great overall health.

This diet is designed as an easy-to-use guideline, helping you to make informed choices about what to eat. It is compatible with most medically supervised diets. However, before starting any diet, check with your physician. Every item listed has met all of the standards established by the USDA, World Health Organization, National Research Council, the American Dietetic Association, and the Surgeon General.

Fruits, vegetables, grains, and supplements are "required" and should be enjoyed every day, as they are the foundation for healthy bowel function. All other foods listed may be eaten in the amounts recommended for a complete diet.

THE BOWEL HEALTH AND COLON CANCER PREVENTION PLAN

FRUITS AND VEGETABLES (REQUIRED)

- Five or more servings daily
- Fruit serving: one piece or one cup
- Vegetable serving: one cup

RECOMMENDED:

(*exceptional cancer and heart disease preventing properties)

FRESH FRUITS

*apricots
*blackberries
*blueberries
*boysenberries
*cranberries
*citrus fruits
dates
figs
*guava
kiwi
*kumquats
*mangoes
*nectarines
pears
*plums
*raspberries
rhubarb (stems only)
starfruit (carambola)
*tomatoes

DRIED FRUITS

*apricots
apples

*cranberries
currants
*peaches
pears
raisins

FRESH VEGETABLES

*artichokes
*asparagus
*beets
*bok choy
*broccoli
*Brussels sprouts
*carrots
*cauliflower
chickpeas
chives
*collard greens
corn
*eggplant
field greens
*garlic
*onions
parsnips
peas
peppers
potatoes (skins)
*spinach
*sweet potatoes
turnips
*winter squash
*yams

TIPS

- Eat raw or lightly cooked until crunchy

- Use low fat cooking techniques: blanching, stir-fry, grilling, or steaming
- Leave peels on whenever possible
- Use quick-frozen when fresh is not available
- Canned fruits or vegetables should be packed in their natural juices; if not, rinse with water before cooking or eating
- Use seasonings to flavor and minimize use of salt: dill, basil, rosemary, cumin, chervil, cilantro, sage, thyme, and cinnamon
- Buy in season for highest quality and best price
- Buy organically grown to reduce exposure to toxins and pesticides

CAUTION
Use prunes only as a tasty addition to your diet. Do not use daily as a laxative, as intestinal injury may occur

GRAINS (REQUIRED)

- Minimum of two servings daily
- Serving: two slices of bread or one bagel or one cup of grain (cereals, rice, corn, pasta)

RECOMMENDED:

BREADS	CEREALS	GRAINS
bran	wheat bran	barley
cracked wheat	corn bran	buckwheat (kasha)
nine grain	rice bran	bulghur

BREADS	CEREALS	GRAINS
oatmeal	oat bran	corn flour (whole grain)
whole wheat	amaranth	corn meal (whole grain)
whole wheat English muffins	quinoa	millet
whole wheat pita	Granola	spelt
pumpernickel	Grapenuts	brown rice
oat bran muffins	Shredded Wheat	wild rice
corn tortillas	Weet-a-bix	couscous
whole wheat tortillas		
rye		

TIPS

- Use a variety, as each grain has a special function and complements the others.
- Grains such as barley, bulghur, and brown rice can be used in soups and stuffings.
- Buckwheat for pancakes or pasta
- Bulghur for tabbouleh or sautéed with vegetables

CAUTION

- Eight glasses of fluid a day must accompany fiber intake
- Avoid “enriched” flours
- Excessive intake of refined grains (white flour) may lead to weight gain

SUPPLEMENTS (REQUIRED DAILY)

- 1-2 iron-free multi-vitamin and mineral tablets (folic acid 400 mcg-1 mg daily)
- 800-1000 units vitamin E
- Maximum 500 mg vitamin C
- 1200 mg calcium
- 4000 mg fish oil
- 81 mg half-strength coated aspirin three times a week

TIPS

- Take minerals at night for maximum absorption
- Take supplements on a full stomach
- Use water when taking supplements

DAIRY

- Maximum of one to two cups of fat-free milk or yogurt (active culture) or four tbsp. of fat-free cheese or two tbsp. low-fat cheese daily
- Maximum of one tbsp. butter or margarine twice a week

TIPS

- Use nonfat milk in all coffee drinks
- Use nonfat or low-fat yogurt, sour cream, or cream cheese instead of butter or margarine when possible
- Skim or 1% fat milk only

PROTEIN

- Two to four egg whites once a week or one to two whole eggs weekly
- One cup peas or beans daily

  OR
- three to six ounces of lean meat, poultry, or fish daily
- Duck or goose on special occasions, once or twice a year

- Mussels, oysters, shrimp, or lobster not more than twice a month

RECOMMENDED:

MEATS	POULTRY	FISH
top round	chicken	salmon
bottom round	turkey	tuna
chuck roast	quail	mackerel
London broil	Cornish game hens	cod
flank steak	ostrich	anchovies
pork tenderloin		sardines
venison		
veal		

TIPS

- Free range or organically fed meats
- "Choice" or "select" grades
- Poultry fed omega-3 feeds
- Use low-fat cooking techniques: braising, grilling, roasting, and steaming
- Add flavors with low-fat stocks or juices rather than cream sauces
- Use bold spices: lemongrass, ginger, or cumin

FATS AND OILS

- Maximum four tbsp. oil or fat daily
- Avoid foods where more than 20% of the total calories are fat (to find this number, divide the total calories per

serving by the calories from fat; an answer of five or greater is acceptable)

- Fried foods may be eaten occasionally, once every two weeks

RECOMMENDED:

canola oil
olive oil (virgin, extra virgin, organic, flavored)
pumpkin seed oil
walnut oil

OCCASIONAL (not more than 1 ounce twice a week)

almond oil
corn oil
safflower oil
sesame oil (plain or toasted)
sunflower oil
soybean oil

MINIMAL (rare occasions, not more than 1 ounce a month)

apricot kernel oil
avocado oil
bacon fat
butter (all types)
coconut oil
cottonseed oil
filbert oil
hazelnut oil
lard
margarine
palm and palm kernel oil
peanut oil
pinenut oil
schmaltz (rendered chicken fat)
shortening
vegetable oil

TIPS

- Read labels carefully for fats and oils used
- Never reuse oil after cooking
- Use nonstick cookware
- Saturated fats are fats that are solid at room temperature
- Always use low or nonfat products

CAUTION

Avoid partially hydrogenated or hydrogenated (saturated) oils, as they are converted into trans fatty acids upon cooking; trans fatty acids have been implicated in the causation of cancer and coronary artery disease. They are listed under MINIMAL.

SWEETS

- Maximum of one 2-ounce serving daily
- Low-fat or fat free ice cream or frozen yogurt serving: 1/2 cup
- Sorbet serving: 1/2 cup

TIPS

- Use fresh fruits as toppings
- Low-fat baked goods made with preferred grains
- Cakes, pies, and pastries on special occasions only
- Avoid high fructose corn syrup in foods and beverages

ALCOHOL

- Maximum of two 4 ounce glasses of wine (red preferred) **OR**
- 12 oz. beer (light preferred) **OR**
- 1 1/4 oz. hard liquor daily

FLUIDS

In order to form stools that are easy to pass and to clear toxins from the body, an average of eight glasses of fluid should be consumed daily. The type of fluid is very important. Water, juices, and soups are preferred, but caffeinated drinks such as coffee, tea, or chocolate and alcoholic beverages are excluded since they are diuretics. It's all right to have these drinks in moderation, they just don't count toward your daily fluid requirement. A simple way to achieve your fluid intake is by drinking a little at a time, spread throughout the day. A good bottled water is preferred. Take it with you in the car, in your briefcase, in a purse, or a backpack. It can be left on your desk to sip during the day or by your bed at night.

Juices, soups, and smoothies are effective ways to meet your fluid requirements, and have cancer and disease preventing properties. Read the label carefully to avoid products with high fructose corn syrup and carbonated drinks—they can produce gas and weight gain.

SUGGESTIONS

- Spread fluid intake throughout the day
- Take your water with you
- Every time you get in or out of your car, take a sip
- Sip while reading or watching TV
- Keep a bottle of water at your bedside
- Remember to drink before, during and after exercising
- Don't wait till you are thirsty to have a drink
- Drinking water before a meal also helps you to lose weight

RECOMMENDED FLUIDS

(*exceptional cancer and heart disease preventing properties
Water)

JUICES

apple
*apricot nectar
banana
blueberry
*boysenberry
*carrot
cherry
*cranberry
grape
*grapefruit
guava
kiwi
*lemon
*lime
*mango nectar
*orange
*papaya nectar
passionfruit nectar
peach nectar
pear nectar
pineapple
*raspberry
strawberry nectar
tangerine
*vegetable juice (V-8)
watermelon

CAUTION
Prune juice only occasionally. Daily use as a laxative can damage the bowels.

DAIRY AND DAIRY SUBSTITUTES

acidophilus milk
goat milk
kefir
Lact-Aid
milk (low-fat or fat free)
*multi-grain drink
*oat drink
rice drink
*smoothies (nonfat)
soy milk
sport drinks
yogurt drinks (active cultures)

TEAS

chai
chamomile
ginger
gingko
ginseng
*green tea
herbal teas
decaffeinated teas

EXERCISE

Exercise helps to promote motility of the bowel muscles, emptying of the stomach, and normal pressures in the colon. It improves your cardiac output and circulation to the entire body and relieves stress.

Physicians have recognized constipation as a common problem of the inactive person. Even if you were to relax, take fluids, and eat a healthy diet, you could still have problems with your bowels if you did not exercise.

Now, you don't have to be a jock to get the proper exercise; there are many easy ways to get your body moving and keep it moving throughout the day. Any exercise is good, and regular exercise helps the heart work more efficiently, improves stamina, and helps control diabetes, blood pressure, and cholesterol. Brisk exercise for thirty minutes three times a week is all that is necessary. Remember, you are toning and conditioning your bowel and your entire body to easily handle the myriad of stresses that life has in store for us all.

SUGGESTIONS

- aerobics
- biking
- dancing
- gym workout
- jogging
- rollerblading
- sports
- swimming
- walking
- T'ai chi
- yoga

RELAXATION

Don't obsess about having a bowel movement. It's not the end of the world if you don't have a b.m. every day! There are many reasons why this can happen. The normal frequency of bowel movements ranges from three a day to three a week, as long as you do not have to strain. Take some time away from the hectic routine of daily life. This is what we call "being good to yourself!" Every single day, if only for a few minutes, set aside time for yourself to relax and have a good gentle movement.

SUGGESTIONS

- Take a leisurely bath. Try some aromatic candles, bath salts, and oils.
- Listen to music
- Meditate
- Spend time alone
- Do yoga or stretching
- Spend time outdoors
- Do deep breathing exercises
- Daydream
- Have a massage
- Laugh (our personal favorite, and highly underrated)

THE BOWEL HEALTH AND COLON CANCER PREVENTION PLAN

SAMPLE MENUS

SUNDAY

MORNING	buckwheat pancakes with blueberries and maple syrup orange juice water decaf coffee or skim milk or herbal tea
MID-MORNING	dried fruits
MID-DAY	roast beef sandwich with whole grain bread, lettuce, onion, tomato, and low-fat mayo carrot salad with raisins water lemonade or iced herbal tea
SNACK	fruit smoothie
EVENING	grilled salmon fresh spinach sauté with olive oil and garlic baked potato with low-fat sour cream and chives tomato salad with fresh basil lemon sorbet water decaf coffee or tea

MONDAY

MORNING	shredded wheat sliced peaches skim or low-fat milk water decaf coffee or herbal tea
MID-MORNING	fruit juice
MID-DAY	vegetable soup Romaine lettuce salad with anchovies, lemon and olive oil dressing whole grain roll water iced decaf tea or specialty decaf coffee
SNACK	pear
EVENING	roasted chicken with wild rice stuffing and dried cranberries steamed broccoli with lemon juice low-fat vanilla ice cream with fresh strawberries water decaf coffee or tea

TUESDAY

MORNING	grapefruit whole grain toast with boysenberry preserves water decaf nonfat specialty coffee
MID-MORNING	fruit smoothie
MID-DAY	tuna fish salad sandwich on rye bread with watercress and tomato apricot nectar or fresh apricots water decaf coffee or tea
SNACK	apple
EVENING	grilled marinated flank steak couscous with dried fruits and spring onion sautéed red and yellow peppers in olive oil and garlic raspberry low-fat frozen yogurt water decaf coffee or tea

WEDNESDAY

MORNING	oatmeal with currants and walnuts skim milk apple juice water decaf coffee or tea
MID-MORNING	decaf nonfat specialty coffee
MID-DAY	vegetarian wrap (burrito) with whole wheat flour tortilla, beans, salsa, and rice water fruit drink
SNACK	V-8 juice
EVENING	pasta primavera (spring vegetables) field greens salad with low-fat Italian dressing mixed fruit compote water decaf coffee or tea

THURSDAY

MORNING	papaya with lime toasted whole wheat bagel with low-fat cream cheese orange juice water decaf nonfat specialty coffee
MID-MORNING	yogurt
MID-DAY	mushroom barley soup spinach salad with low-fat sherry dressing whole wheat crackers water herbal tea
SNACK	baked low-fat chips
EVENING	pork tenderloin grilled with mustard sauce grilled corn on the cob glazed carrots marinated green bean salad low-fat oatmeal cookie water decaf coffee or tea

FRIDAY

MORNING	oat bran muffin melon pineapple juice water herbal tea
MID-MORNING	dried fruit
MID-DAY	vegetarian chili baked low-fat tortilla chips salsa water decaf coffee nonfat specialty coffee
SNACK	fruit juice
EVENING	broiled tuna with mango relish roasted red potatoes with garlic and rosemary steamed asparagus with lemon whole grain roll mixed berry compote water decaf coffee or tea

SATURDAY

MORNING	egg white omelet with tomato, basil, and onion whole grain toast prune juice water decaf coffee or tea
MID-MORNING	low-fat fig bar
MID-DAY	chilled artichoke with low-fat dressing walnut wheat bread fruit salad water iced herbal tea
SNACK	cranberry juice
EVENING	pot roast with root vegetables (turnips, carrots, parsnips, and potato) arugula salad with lemon and olive oil pumpernickel roll tropical fruit sorbet water decaf coffee or tea

GLOSSARY

GLOSSARY

ABSORPTION: The uptake of molecules from the digestive tract into the bloodstream.

ANUS: Specialized skin tissue tucked into the pelvic floor, joining the rectum, common site of fissures and hemorrhoids.

ASCENDING COLON: Follows the cecum, courses along the right side of the abdomen under the ribcage and liver

BOLUS: A discrete mass of a substance propelled through a tubular structure.

BOWEL: The intestine, excluding the esophagus and stomach.
Small bowel—small intestine
Large bowel—colon

CECUM: The beginning of the large intestine, or colon; usually located in the lower right part of the abdomen.

CROHN'S DISEASE: An inflammatory condition of the entire bowel, of unknown cause, most commonly involving the end of the small intestine and colon.

CYTOKINE: Chemical messengers secreted by immune defense cells that regulate immune responses, modify most of the functions of cells and tissues in the body.

DESCENDING COLON: The colon coursing down the left side of the abdomen from the splenic flexure to the sigmoid colon.

DIETARY FIBER: Undigestible material from fruits, grains, and vegetables in the diet.

DIGESTION: The breaking down of complex food molecules into smaller units to facilitate absorption.

EXCRETION: The removal of undigested molecules and waste products from the body.

FERMENTATION: The metabolism of food by microorganisms resulting in the production of gases and organic byproducts such as acids.

FISSURE: A tear or crack in a tissue.

GASTROENTEROLOGIST: A physician fully trained in internal medicine with specialized training in the diagnosis and treatment of gastrointestinal and liver disease.

GUT: The entire gastrointestinal tract: esophagus, stomach, small and large intestine.

HEMORRHOID: Dilated vein in the rectum and anus.

HEPATIC FLEXURE: The turn of the ascending colon to the transverse colon under the liver.

HIATUS HERNIA: A protrusion of the upper stomach through the opening of the diaphragm (hiatus) into the chest.

HORMONE: A chemical secreted by a specialized cell or group of cells into the bloodstream to a target tissue to promote or regulate a specific activity in that tissue.

INFLAMMATION: Swelling and irritation in cells, tissues, or organs produced by immune defense cells and their chemical messengers.

INSOLUBLE FIBER: Dietary fiber that becomes incorporated into the solid portion of digestive juice, forms stools, tones intestinal muscles.

MALABSORPTION: The incomplete absorption of food molecules.

MELENA: Black, thick, shiny, malodorous stools indicative of bleeding from the gastrointestinal tract, usually the upper gastrointestinal tract.

MICROORGANISM: A bacterium, virus, protozoan, or fungus visible only through a microscope.

MOTILITY: Coordinated, muscular contractions of the digestive tube.

MUCOSA: The lining cells of the gastrointestinal tract.

MUCUS: A complex molecular material secreted by lining cells of organs as a protective coating.

NEURAL TUBE: Structure on developing embryo that becomes the nervous system in the adult.

PERISTALSIS: The orderly progression of intestinal muscular contractions propelling food or liquid from mouth to anus.

POLYP: A small, discrete group of cells on the bowel mucosa that are growing and dividing more rapidly than their neighboring cells.

PROCTOLOGIST: A surgeon trained in diseases of the rectum and colon.

RECTUM: The straight segment of the colon in the pelvis which connects the sigmoid colon to the anus. Site of specialized sensors and muscles controlling stool evacuation.

SCYBALA: A rock-hard round pellet stool.

SECRETION: The transport of a molecule from a cell in response to a signal or stimulus.

SIGMOID COLON: The colon in the left lower portion of the abdomen, commonly a site of high pressure.

SOLUBLE FIBER: Fiber that becomes incorporated into the liquid portion of the digestive juices, a major energy source for the large intestine; a secondary source for the small intestine.

SPHINCTER: A specialized group of muscles that control the diameter or opening of a tubular structure.

SPLENIC FLEXURE: The turn of the transverse colon under the spleen in the left upper abdomen, downward to the descending colon.

STOOL: Fecal material.

STRICTURE (STENOSIS): A narrowing in the digestive (or any tubular structure) tube caused by scar tissue in response to injury or inflammation.

TENESMUS: A sudden, jolt-like pain in the rectum, often associated with irritation of the rectum from various causes.

TOXIN: A molecule produced by a microorganism that affects cellular function in the body.

TRANSVERSE COLON: The portion of the colon from the right upper abdomen to the left upper abdomen; commonly distends with gas.

ULCERATIVE COLITIS: An inflammatory condition of unknown cause involving the colon.

REFERENCES

REFERENCES

General Reference

Gastrointestinal Disease. Sleisenger M, Fordtran J, Scharschmidt B, Feldman M, eds. W. B. Saunders Co. (Philadelphia), 6th edition 1998.

The Mind-Bowel Relationship

1. Aziz Q, Thompson DG. Brain-gut axis in health and disease. Gastroenterology 1998; 114:559-578.
2. Mayer EA, Murakata J, Chang L. Does mind-body medicine have a role in gastroenterology? Curr Opin Gastroent 1998; 13:1-4.

Gas

1. Suarez FL, Furne JK, Springfield JR, Levitt MD. Identification of gases responsible for the odor of human flatus and evaluation of a device purported to reduce this odor (abstr). Gastroenterology 1997: 112:A45.

Polyp-Cancer Sequence

1. Itzkowitz S, Kim YS. Polyps and benign neoplasms of the colon. *In* Gastrointestinal Disease. Sleisenger M and Fordtran J, eds. W. B. Saunders Co. (Philadelphia) 1993, pp 1402-1430.
2. Correa P. Epidemiology of polyps and cancer. *In* The pathogenesis of colorectal cancer. Morson BC, ed. W. B. Saunders Co. (Philadelphia), 1978.

Fiber

1. Burkitt DP. Epidemiology of cancer of the colon and rectum. Cancer 1971: 28:3-13.

2. Potter JD. Fiber and colorectal cancer—where to now? New Engl J Med 1999; 340:223-224.
3. Howe GR, Benito E, Castelleto R et al. Dietary intake of fiber and decreased risk of cancers of the colon and rectum: Evidence from the combined analysis of 13 case-control studies. J Natl Cancer Inst 1992: 84:1887-1896.

Folic Acid and Multiple Vitamins

1. Giovanucci E, Stampfer MJ, Colditz GA et al. Multivitamin use, folate, and colon cancer in women in the nurses' health study. Ann Int Med 1998: 129:517-524.

Fat

1. Armstrong B, Doll R. Environmental factors and cancer incidence and mortality in different countries, with special reference to dietary practices. Int J Cancer 1975; 15: 617-631.
2. Reddy BS, Cohen LA, McCoy GD et al. Nutrition and its relationship to cancer. Adv Cancer Res 1980; 32:237.
3. Giovanucci E, Stampfer MJ et al. Relationship of diet to risk of colorectal adenoma in men. J Natl Cancer Inst 1992; 84:91.

Fat, Fiber, Meat, and Fish

1. Willett WC, Stampfer MJ, Colditz GA et al. Relationship of meat, fat, and fiber intake to the risk of colon cancer in a prospective study among women. New Engl J Med 1990; 323:1664-1672.

Fish Oils

1. Wargovich MJ. Fish oils and colon cancer. Gastroenterology 1992; 103:1096-1098.
2. Blot WJ, Lancer A, Fraumeni JF et al. Cancer mortality among Alaska natives, 1960-69. J Natl Cancer Inst 1975; 55:547-554.

3. Anti M, Marra G, Armelao F et al. Effect of n-3 fatty acids on rectal mucosal cell proliferation in subjects at risk for colon cancer. Gastroenterology 1992; 103:883-891.

Aspirin

1. Ladabaum V, Sowers M. Potential population-wide impact of aspirin on colon cancer mortality. Gastroenterology 1998; 115:514-515.
2. Thun MJ, Namboordini NM, Heath CWJ. Aspirin use and reduced risk of fatal colon cancer. New Engl J Med 1991; 325:1593-1596.
3. Greenberg ER, Baron JA, Freeman DHJ et al. Reduced risk of large bowel adenomas among aspirin users: The Polyp Prevention Study Group. J Natl Cancer Inst 1993; 85:912-916.

Calcium, Vitamin E, Vitamin C

1. Alberts D, Titenbaugh C, Story J et al. Randomized, double-blinded, placebo-controlled study of effect of wheat bran fiber and calcium on fecal bile acids in patients with resected adenomatous colon polyps. J Natl Cancer Inst 1996; 88:81-92.
2. Baron JA, Beach M, Mandel JS et al. Calcium supplements for the prevention of colorectal adenomas. New Engl J Med 1999; 340:101-107.
3. Hofstad B, Almendingen K, Vatu M et al. Growth and recurrence of colorectal polyps: A double-blind 3-year intervention with calcium and antioxidants. Digestion 1998; 59:148-156.
4. Bostick RM, Potter JD, McKenzie DR et al. Reduced risk of colon cancer with high intake of vitamin E: The Iowa Women's Health Study. Cancer Res 1993; 53:4230-4237.
5. Pritchard RS, Baron JA, Deverdier MG. Dietary calcium, vitamin D, and the risk of colorectal cancer in Stockholm,

Sweden. Cancer Epidem Biomark and Prevention 1996; 5:897-900.

<u>Colonoscopy</u>

1. American Gastroenterologic Association. Screening for colorectal cancer: Guidelines and rationale. Gastroenterology 1997; 112:594-642.
2. Winauer SJ, Zauber AG, Ho MN et al. Prevention of colorectal cancer by colonoscopic polypectomy: The National Polyp Study Workgroup. New Engl J Med 1993; 329:1977-1981.

About the Authors

Jeffrey M. Aron, M.D. is the chairman of the Nutritional Support Committee and an assistant clinical professor of medicine at the University of California Medical Center in San Francisco. He has been in the practice of gastroenterology for the last 26 years, and has served as the chairman of the Division of Gastroenterology and Nutrition at Mount Zion Medical Center for 19 years. Dr. Aron is a graduate of UCLA, and earned his medical degree from the University of California at Irvine, where he co-founded the school newspaper, *The Impulse*. Currently he serves on the Medical Advisory Board of the Crohn's Colitis Foundation of America, and was a founding member of the Northern California Chapter of the American Society for Parenteral and Enteral Nutrition. He has lectured and taught at major national and international conferences, and has contributed to numerous scientific publications, including the book Nutrition and AIDS.

Dr. Aron and his wife Harriette reside in San Francisco, and are the parents of a son.

Printed in the United States
5534